"*Beyond Guilt Trips* is a fantastic guide ̶ ̶ ̶ ̶ ̶ ̶ ̶ ̶ ̶ ̶ ̶ ̶ ̶ ̶ ̶ ence in productive ways."

— Timothy Longman, associate professor of Political Science and International Relations, Boston University

"Though there are many books and guides that discuss the importance of being good eco-travelers, there are few that help us to be good "anthro-travelers." *Beyond Guilt Trips* takes us deep into that world, providing tools for deeper awareness and engagement during our interactions with unfamiliar cultures and individuals. Taranath helps us to navigate our inner and outer journeys, and to return home with a profoundly enriched view of our world."

— Jeff Greenwald, author of *The Size of the World*, director of EthicalTraveler.org

"Over the past twenty years I've led groups on tours and explored the globe on my own, travelling to over fifty countries. The search for deeper meaning is consistent through it all. Taranath is an expert at recognizing deeply felt issues and providing an approach that is inclusive and fulfilling. Let her be your guide through whatever travels you have ahead!"

— Ben Cameron, Rick Steves' Europe tour guide

"This is the guide I wished I'd had when first starting to travel the world as a young person. Packed with wisdom and useful tips, *Beyond Guilt Trips* should be in all campus libraries, youth hostels, and community organizations."

— Faith Adiele, author of *Meeting Faith* and founder of VONA Travel Writing

"Taranath skillfully blends storytelling with a guidebook approach to how we can all travel better—go beyond good intentions and become intentional travelers. A much-needed book to transform the travelscape."

—Amy Gigi Alexander, editor-in-chief, *Panorama: the Journal of Intelligent Travel*

"Taranath illuminates perspectives that many of us seldom consider but are vital to our understanding of our neighbors and ourselves, both at home and abroad."

—Larry Habegger, executive editor, Travelers' Tales Books

"I am so grateful for this book, for it left me reflecting on the one trip we are all on, traveling through this life! Taranath is an excellent and humble storyteller who teaches us through stories. Readers will find nuggets here that will help us all to be our best selves."

—Michele E. Storms, executive director, American Civil Liberties Union, Washington State

"Anu's writing never sugarcoats, but helps us speak about unequal structures, uncomfortable facts, and our own positions as we travel five or five thousand miles from what's familiar. This isn't just a book to read; it's a way to walk in the world."

—Dr. Peter Moran, former director, University of Washington Study Abroad Office

"At a time when it has become radical to ask ourselves what it means to be who we are, where we are, *Beyond Guilt Trips* holds space for these conversations where there wasn't any before."

—Bani Amor, queer travel writer

"*Beyond Guilt Trips* offers a consciousness-raising for travelers, even as it shows us ways to stay present and compassionate amidst a sea of potential confusion, doubt, and guilt."

—Laurie Hovell McMillin, editor of *Away Journal*

"Taranath offers the reader sympathetic understanding while firmly naming the realities and complexities of the unjust societies we inhabit and create. While she does not let us off the hook, she consistently brings us back to our shared humanity. I wish this book had been available when I first began to travel abroad."

—Tina Lopes, co-author of *Dancing On Live Embers: Challenging Racism in Organizations*

"Taranath unflinchingly confronts the awkward feelings of guilt, shame, and privilege that inevitably arise from international (and even inter-neighborhood) travel, and somehow manages to stare them down, deconstruct them, and take away their power. *Beyond Guilt Trips* is an essential companion to all those leading, engaging in, or contemplating travel, to ensure they will embark on an inward journey that mirrors the outward one."

—Claire Bennett, co-author of *Learning Service: The Essential Guide to Volunteer Travel*

"*Beyond Guilt Trips* is part reflective memoir, part ethnographic deep-dive, and part user manual for navigating our increasingly unequal world. . . This book is certainly the most teachable—and instructive—book on global travel I have read yet."

—David Citrin, Global Health and Anthropology, University of Washington

"*Beyond Guilt Trips* unpacks some of the biggest racial and cultural issues facing Westerners traveling abroad. In straightforward language, Taranath addresses white privilege, micro-aggressions, inequality, and the unspoken rules of race and economics that travelers face when visiting foreign cultures. Simple, necessary, and razor-sharp, this book is an accessible and friendly guide for anyone interested in learning how to 'sit with discomfort.'"

—Adriana Paramo, author of *Looking for Esperanza and My Mother's Funeral*

"When Mark Twain observed that travel was fatal to bigotry and narrow-mindedness, he somehow predicted we would have this wise and timely book in hand. Taranath shows us how to build a toolbox of keen observation, respectful engagement, and honest examination as we move among our neighborhoods as well as through our world."

—David Fenner, Peace Corps volunteer 1979–82, founding director, World Learning Oman Center, former assistant vice provost for international education, University of Washington

"This book takes us into the heart of where we need to go if we truly aim to do away with injustice and transform the world."

—Michael Westerhaus MD, MA and Amy Finnegan PhD, co-directors, SocMed

"Instead of guilting or shaming people when they become more aware of their privilege or wealth, *Beyond Guilt Trips* brings everyone along without erasing histories of oppression. With a generous spirit, Taranath holds space for both the learning of travelers and the dignity of the people they encounter, offering the possibility of meaningful mutual exchange."

—Frances Lee, writer and cultural activist

Beyond
Guilt Trips

Beyond
Guilt Trips

Mindful Travel in an
Unequal World

- - - - - - - -

Anu Taranath
Illustrated by Ronald "Otts" Bolisay

Between the Lines
Toronto

Beyond Guilt Trips
Mindful Travel in an Unequal World
© 2019 Anu Taranath

First published in 2019 by
Between the Lines
401 Richmond Street West
Studio 281
Toronto, Ontario M5V 3A8
Canada
1-800-718-7201
www.btlbooks.com

Every reasonable effort has been made to identify copyright holders. Between the Lines would be pleased to have any errors or omissions brought to its attention.

Library and Archives Canada Cataloguing in Publication

Taranath, Anu, author
          Beyond guilt trips : mindful travel in an unequal world / by Anu Taranath.

Includes index.
Issued in print and electronic formats.
ISBN 978-1-77113-432-3 (softcover).--ISBN 978-1-77113-433-0 (EPUB).--ISBN 978-1-77113-434-7 (PDF)

          1. Developing countries--Description and travel.
2. Travel--Social aspects. 3. Travel--Moral and ethical aspects.
4. Taranath, Anu--Travel. I. Title.

G151.T37 2019   910.9172'4   C2018-906064-6
                                                       C2018-906065-4

Text and cover design by Maggie Earle
Cover and interior illustrations by Ronald "Otts" Bolisay, https://otts.carbonmade.com
Printed in Canada

We acknowledge for their financial support of our publishing activities: the Government of Canada; the Canada Council for the Arts, which last year invested $153 million to bring the arts to Canadians throughout the country; and the Government of Ontario through the Ontario Arts Council, the Ontario Book Publishers Tax Credit program, and Ontario Creates.

Education does not make us educable. It is our awareness of being unfinished that makes us educable.

—PAULO FREIRE, *PEDAGOGY OF FREEDOM: ETHICS, DEMOCRACY AND CIVIC COURAGE*

The learning process is something you can incite, literally incite, like a riot.

—AUDRE LORDE, *SISTER OUTSIDER*

Planes carry passengers. What passengers carry on their consciences, their guilt, grievances, goodwill is hard to say.

—ROMESH GUNESEKERA, *NOONTIDE TOLL*

CONTENTS

PROLOGUE

_ _ _ _ _ _ _ _ _ _ _ _ _ _ _ _ _

Beyond Guilt Trips: Practical Application for Travelers

Toni Morrison wrote, "If there's a book that you want to read, but it hasn't been written yet, then you must write it." I took Ms. Morrison's sentiment to heart, and this is that book. As I began to write, I recorded the kinds of discomforting feelings I and many Western travelers I know experienced, but hadn't seen represented in a book form. I pictured my reader: a well-intentioned young adult from the West who travels to low-income countries in the Global South. This person feels sensitivity and curiosity for others, though hasn't necessarily had much exposure to or experience with conversations about identity, race, diversity, and equity; access to resources; structural oppression; and how all these issues might play out in people's lives.

During the writing and research process, I began to realize that the guilt and discomfort we may experience abroad on account of the differences in race, resources, and culture oftentimes mimic the guilt and discomfort we may experience much closer to home as we move through different neighborhoods and communities, or even work with different kinds of people. Put differently, experiencing guilt and discomfort when we're far away from home and experiencing guilt and discomfort when we're nearer to home are all instances of difficult-to-navigate feelings that can be useful to unpack, process, and reflect upon. These feelings are connected in many ways and originate from similar historical processes that have to do with identity, power, and social hierarchies. So while this book is for you if you're, say, embarking on a study abroad program to South Africa or currently in the middle of your governmental or NGO volunteer placement in Cameroon, this book is also for you if you're a student in the West enrolled in a service-learning course. It's for you if you're preparing to do field research abroad or community-based research and scholarship closer to home, engaged in faith-based service projects at home or abroad, or interning in an afterschool program or a local non-profit focused on providing resources to disadvantaged populations in your town or city.

You need not, though, have traveled, volunteered, or even be a student to find something useful in these pages. This book can be a resource if you're craving productive conversation on diversity, equity, and identity issues as part of staff professional development in your public agency, school district, library system, company, or firm. If you've got a "diversity, equity, and inclusion" committee at your workplace or are having diversity challenges of many sorts, this could be a suitable book to inspire constructive dialogue and model conversation. It could even be useful for your school or college as a common text to read and discuss if you're part of a campus-wide "day of service," like the one typically held in the United States on Martin Luther King Jr. Day every January, or Canada's National Volunteer Week held yearly in April. Though most of the examples I've used throughout the book relate to international travel, the underlying issues of who we are and how we might notice and navigate our differences in an unfair world can relate to any of us, both at home and abroad.

Though this isn't a typical memoir, I often describe my own experiences as a way to invite you to consider your own journeys from a broader perspective. Throughout the book, you'll also hear from a wide range of student travelers who reflect on their journeys across race and class in lands both far and near. Though I've often used pseudonyms and changed identifying details, all the stories you'll read are based on true experiences. Some stories focus on my own travels with groups of students or on my own. Some draw from conversations I've had with travelers, tourists, program directors, group leaders, volunteers, and students traveling abroad; others draw from student assignments, focus groups, email correspondence, or field report journals.

Politics of Care

It might be helpful to say a bit about where this book is located politically and socially. All of my work is embedded in a politics of care, transformative social change, and deep justice for both ourselves and others. When I think about my ideal vision for how our society should be, I'd like to see a society in which all people enjoy the benefits and riches of a quality life, not just those who have power, wealth,

educational access, a particular skin color or body shape. I'd like a society in which we can all love who we'd like to love and look how we'd like to look. A society where all of us enjoy good nutrition and healthcare, green trees, and warm homes. A society in which kids play and read books and where all of us feel heard,

seen, and validated. I'd like a society in which we all have enough—not just a few of us, but all of us.

Our world though is not set up like this. The sad truth of our status quo is that too many of us—both in our own communities and around the world—feel ostracized and live without enough of too many things: opportunity, safety, peace, and security. Many of us want to remedy these problems, and so we work for social justice in both small and big ways. We investigate and question the "business-as-usual" status quo, search for ways to be more equitable, and forge paths toward personal and community wellbeing. When we critically notice our surroundings and ask questions about how systems of power confer advantages for some and difficulties for others, we practice the first steps toward interrupting unfair systems. When more of us wonder why business-as-usual often means more opportunity, safety, peace, and security for fewer of us we build a stronger movement for accountability and change.

Movements for peace and justice must dismantle unfair power structures, but must also prioritize loving relationships between people. My sense of justice work is compassion-based and intensely local, no matter where in the world I might be. My approach is similar to Frances Lee's, a scholar who writes about activist culture: "I believe in 'yes and' methods of justice work; yes, a historical system of oppression operates in our society that results in mass inequity and harm, and we all have the capacity to recognize the humanity in each other and forge genuine connections." Justice work for me is not only about working to change what is ugly and unequal in society; it is also about going deep into our own personal stories to be more in tune with ourselves, our values, and heartfelt alignment.

Whether you picked up this book on your own or you've been asked to read it by a teacher, program leader, colleague, or professor, the fact that you are holding it signals to me your willingness to consider and engage with the ideas presented. While I won't sugarcoat things to artificially sweeten the tough parts (because that's not good teaching), please know that I will not shame or blame you for particular features like your race, wealth, gender, being raised in a high-income country, or anything you do not control. Maya Angelou has said, "I've learned that people will forget what you said, people will forget what you did, but people will never forget how you made them feel." In my opinion, shame and blame can be useful tools for political movements, but they do not constitute good teaching and often do not result in good learning. Shame, in fact, corrodes our connections to one another and keeps us isolated. *Beyond Guilt Trips* is meant to do the exact opposite. I will not shame and blame you for any of your identities and advantages and, rather, will ask you to question your own experiences and place in the world. Together, we can work on transforming our guilt trips across difference into more productive explorations about ourselves and each other.

Though *Beyond Guilt Trips* has been foremost on my mind the last few years, I know this book—or any book, really—cannot shift society. A book's value is only as good as the people who engage with it. Therein lies our potential. James Baldwin's words come to mind: "You write in order to change the world, knowing perfectly well that you probably can't, but also knowing that literature is indispensable to the world. . . . The world changes according to the way people see it, and if you alter, even by a millimeter, the way . . . people look at reality, then you can change it."

CHAPTER 1

- -

Before You Buy Your Ticket, Read This

Making Connections: Identity and Difference

I BROUGHT MY FOUR-AND-A-HALF-YEAR-OLD DAUGHTER TO A COMMU-
nity space called Third Place Commons to hear a gospel choir perform
on a Sunday afternoon. My kid and I thread our way through the
crowd. I lead, her little hand grasping my shirt as a leash. We find a
small opening near the front of the stage toward the side. I lift her up
so she can see over the heads around us, and together we notice a few
children dancing to the music, their parents nearby smiling proudly.

My daughter and I sway to the rhythm, and intermittently she
pulls my head toward her to share comments into my ear. From our
vantage point, it seems that the two rows of choir members are com-
prised mostly of Black women, a few Black men, a few Asian American
women, and two or three white women. Robust and energetic, the
choir director rouses her singers and audience alike with energy and
poise. I wonder what it would be like to sing in this choir under the

directorship of a charismatic woman of color like her. In all the choirs I've sung in for over eighteen years, I've always stood out as one of a handful of singers of color, and all of my directors and conductors have been white. I ponder auditioning for the gospel choir up on stage.

My daughter wriggles out of my arms. She stands by me for a moment and then joins the dancers in front of the stage. The children twirl and giggle, and their bodies move to the beats of the choir punctuated by shouts of exuberant praise: "Glory!" "Hallelujah!" My kid ambles back toward me and climbs up in my arms, her attention now shifted to the audience. It seems that the seventy or so people around us are all white men and women, mostly elders with various health aides beside them like canes, wheelchairs, and oxygen tanks. They smile and tap their feet. I find myself wondering if so many older white people have come specifically to hear the gospel choir, or if they are the regular Sunday crowd, appreciating whichever live music group has come to perform. I slowly pan the audience and try to discern individual features and attributes of the people all around me, a strategy I use to stay present and aware of the different kinds of differences that might be around me even when there isn't much racial diversity. The joy of the music pours into my heart, and I watch my daughter alternate her focus from the audience to the choir. It's as if she's at a tennis match: her head snaps this way and that.

Suddenly, my kid shimmies down my body and runs into the audience. I'm surprised at her energy, and am curious as to who or what has compelled this sudden burst. Has she recognized someone we know? Our neighbor, perhaps? I crane my head to take a look at who or what she has found. And then I see.

A Black man and woman have just entered and found seats on the other side of the room. Their Blackness is significant because they are the only other visible people of color in the room besides the choir members, my daughter, and me. My daughter stands right smack in front of them with a big smile on her face. I think about calling her name to wave her back, unsure why she's parked herself in front of them and worried if she is bothering them. The couple, though, seems to not mind her presence. Though they are unfamiliar to us, I'm surprised to see how easy and comfortable my kid is with them, as if she's known them her whole life. What happened to all those stranger-danger talks we've had? She waves, and the couple waves back. She claps to the music, and they clap with her. Clearly, they are amused by her attention. The three of them laugh and dance and wiggle their bodies to the music together, happy in each other's company.

After a few moments, the man looks around for a parent, a guardian, a relative—anyone who will claim this child. I wave across the room, and we catch glances and smile in greeting. There is relief in his eyes: oh good, he will not have to take this child home. He resumes his play with my daughter with more vigor now that she has been identified as mine. As the audience breaks into applause at the end of a song, my daughter rushes back to me. She yanks my neck and pulls my ear down to share her big news. "Ammi, Ammi! They are brown too—the same color as us!" She says this not in English but in Kannada, the language she and I speak together. To demonstrate her point, she methodically points to three pieces of evidence: the couple sitting across the room, my brown arm, and then hers. The few white people standing near me haven't understood what she's said, but they've seen my daughter point. I watch them as they follow her finger. Their eyes register a moment of surprise when the point lands on the Black couple, and they quickly look away. I immediately feel a combination of defensiveness, embarrassment, and discomfort. Do the people around me think my child is being rude or racist by pointing to the only Black audience members? Come to think of it, do I think she's being rude? Is she being racist? Tangled, my thoughts wander. Wait, what does being rude or racist really mean? Her statement about us being the same color is honest and merely factual. What's wrong with that, I wonder? She simply said what she saw, and expressed how it made her feel. Acknowledging race is certainly not the same as being racist. Is it somehow wrong for her to feel a connection to the couple across the room? No, I think. That seems ridiculous. Connections on the basis of some shared identity can be a wonderful affirmation of ourselves. You collect manga comic books? So do I! You are from Toronto? Me too! My mind churns: what is honesty and what is rudeness, and who has the power to define the boundaries between the two?

My daughter notices that I've become distracted, and pat-pats my arm a little harder. "Ammi, listen to me! They are also brown!" she says again. I shift my attention from my own ruminations and worries about what the people around me might be thinking back to my kid. I realize that her pat-pats reference race and difference and belonging all at once, and that feels big, expanding my heart in a small way. Before I can say anything to her, she darts back to the couple. The choir belts out a new tune, and the couple and my kid revel in the musical glory.

After the choir takes their final bow, I make my way through the crowd to meet my daughter's new friends. We introduce ourselves and chat about the choir. I tell the couple what my daughter has said about them—"They are brown too!"—and her excitement at this discovery. The man laughs, his large hand resting gently on my daughter's shoulder. "There aren't that many of us brown folks around this part of Seattle, right? Your daughter sure knows what she's talking about." We nod knowingly together and bid each other a warm goodbye.

Noticing Difference–Finding Similarities

Though this scene took place years ago, I've thought about it often. My own questions about what kinds of identities and differences it's okay to notice, when, by whom, and in which context have stayed with me. When my daughter identified with the African American couple solely on the basis of their skin color, she had zero self-consciousness in her actions, no worry that she might be rude, inappropriate, or crossing a possibly discomforting racial boundary. Kids can be more open and less burdened by many of the social stigmas and nervousness that many of us adults bear. These are the grown-up filters about saying or doing "the right thing" that she would, in due course, learn. But as a four-and-a-half-year-old, my kid simply delighted in the recognition of the shared skin color that was so evident and familiar—and used it as a way to connect.

I appreciate too how the couple graciously received my daughter's attention, especially as some of the few people of color in a roomful of white people. Sometimes it's not always comfortable or easy being somewhat different in a gathering of more-alike-ness, especially when it comes to race. We might feel over-visible and on display, and wonder: "What will people think of me? How should I act? I better try to fit in and not bring more attention to myself." The couple could have felt embarrassed by my daughter's obvious attention and brushed her away, but they didn't. They simply enjoyed the moment, outwardly unconcerned by what others might have thought. Their open attitude sent a powerful message to my daughter about it being okay to not only pay attention and notice who's in the room but to speak it aloud. Their openness validated her quite natural desire to find a sense of belonging within people that looked more like her. The interaction also gave me a tangible moment from which to consider how sometimes our desire to be polite or safe and not ruffle feathers associated with identity and difference might make us miss a beautiful connection, however brief and fleeting.

Many of us have grown up believing that noticing difference—differentiating—means we are somehow being unfair, rude, discriminatory, or just plain wrong. We're often in the in-between-space of not knowing if we should be noticing the differences that we notice, and not knowing how to feel about what it is we are noticing. So many of us have been socialized to remain silent, anxious, and sometimes unaware of how our identities have been constructed in relation to other people's identities. We might feel that if we don't talk about race and other differences, we are being polite or tolerant. When you or I see differences between ourselves and others, we might be tempted to downplay these differences: "We are actually all just human. Let's focus on our similarities." Some of us even say, "I am colorblind. I don't care if someone is red, purple or polka-dotted. I see all people just as people."

There is something sweet about wanting to imagine that we are all more similar than different, that our essential humanity brings us together, and the West is a melting pot of people and cultures. And yet, let's consider: if our differences actually could be downplayed, why aren't they in our society? Why are the differences between us still so powerful, salient, and visceral? Why do our differences still make us feel a range of complex feelings, even if we are all collectively human?

Differences, of course, aren't just superficial identifiers. We cannot ignore differences away when those differences structure our material lives in real ways, offering opportunities and benefits for some and making life more difficult and sometimes unsafe and near impossible for others. Because our differences continue to matter greatly in a world that is hierarchical and structurally unequal, we need to get better at addressing them. As sociologist and race scholar Eduardo Bonilla-Silva writes bitingly about the United States, "The melting pot never included people of color. Blacks, Chinese, Puerto Ricans, etc., could not melt into the pot. They could be used as wood to produce the fire for the pot, but they could not be used as material to be melted into the pot."

The first step is admitting that, yes, we notice different identities. The second step is insisting that, no, noticing isn't necessarily bad. Many of us are not even sure how to admit to these seemingly simple steps, for we've been taught to associate differences in identity with discomfort. All of us notice all kinds of things about the people around us, but we're not sure how to think or feel about this. If we can't even productively admit to the noticeable differences we all already notice, I'm not sure how we will ever have the conversations we need to have about the legacies of slavery, imperial-

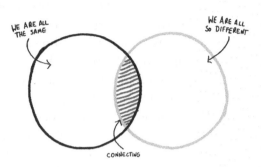

ism, colonialism, and uneven investments in our different communities and what this means for us all. We need to face the ways that these traumatic legacies have warped our conversations about different identities and experiences away from honest openness and more toward silencing discomfort, defensiveness, or other unproductive reactions. This is true especially for those of us who are more advantaged and least affected by the material consequences of this history.

When we recognize that differences between us sometimes matter greatly, we do not necessarily preclude the conditions for connecting. Rather, my belief is that we can connect even better if we learn to acknowledge and reduce the discomfort that usually accompanies interactions across identity, society, and different experiences. Our physical differences and characteristics are right there in front of us all, on display, ordering our world into like-me and not-like-me. I can't look at my colleague with long hair who uses a wheelchair and not see her wheelchair or her long hair. Or look at the thin Latinx man in the gray suit standing behind me in the grocery store line and not see that he's a thin Latinx man in a gray suit. Pretending to not see race and other physical features—or not acknowledging that we see what we see—is an inauthentic and simplistic strategy to actually deal with race and other differences, and speaks volumes about the anxieties present in society. It also leaves us more vulnerable to implicit bias, a discussion coming up in the next section.

As comedian Hari Kondabolu says, "'I don't see race' is essentially saying 'I don't see the uniqueness of your experience and the potential difficulties you face. Also, I am a liar.'" Do we see and register the differences between us? Yes. Should we see and register *only* the differences between us? No. Our differences are both present and real, and they influence our lives in concrete ways. It's also true that our differences may not always be the most important thing about us. Pat Parker's poem "To the White Person Who Wants to be My Friend," begins with this spot-on instruction: "The first thing you do is to forget that I'm Black. Second, you must never forget that I'm Black." To honestly address each of us with dignity and better understand our complex society, we'll need to bravely do both: notice our real differences, *and* also know that our differences might not be everything.

In-Groups and Out-Groups

I wonder if the color connection my daughter felt with the Black couple at the choir concert might be similar to how, say, white Canadian or American backpackers traveling through Barbados or Jamaica might meet each other in a restaurant and develop close bonds over a relatively short period of time. Something about the recognition of sameness and the familiarity it engenders—the experience of being more-alike in a more-different environment—can be extremely seductive to us. It can make us feel seen and validated. How we feel in both contexts matters, whether you're a small kid at a choir show near home or you're a student traveler from Calgary finding others like you in the Caribbean. Noticing who's around us and how that makes us feel isn't a passive act, but rather, an act of agency. The flip-side of cozy and validating in-group connections are, of course, raw out-group discrimination and malicious bias, sometimes on a personal level, sometimes systematic and widespread. Being able to speak aloud the nuances of identity can help clarify for us when it's comforting to focus on our similarities in the midst of difference, and when it's actually narrow minded.

When I think of why my daughter sprinted off toward the Black couple at the gospel choir show, I also think of implicit biases, those unconscious ways we make sense of our world, order it, and divide people into categories of like me or unlike me. Implicit biases and preferences toward our own in-groups can help explain our unconscious preference for or comfort with people like us. Our unconscious behavior too tilts toward our in-group members, bestowing subtle advantages. We might offer more sympathy to people in our in-groups, give each other the benefit of the doubt, have greater trust and empathy with, and feel more comfortable with the unstated rules. With out-group members, our unconscious mind withholds these subtle advantages and instead replaces them with subtle disadvantages: we might be harsher in our judgements, be less forgiving, and feel more discomfort with the unstated rules between people from different groups. Even when we do not consciously intend to discriminate or give subtle disadvantages to members of out-groups, we unconsciously might treat each other differently based on our identities and perceived and visual differences. I wonder: was that what happened with my daughter at the choir show? Did she act on her unconscious preferences to find a more-like-me connection with the Black couple based on similar skin colors? Perhaps so, but it's hard to know for sure. While I don't think she viewed the white elders around us in a particularly negative way, she might have thought the Black couple was "more like us," more like what she was familiar with at home and in her intimate sphere.

As we become better at noticing and understanding what our different identities mean in society both close to home and when we

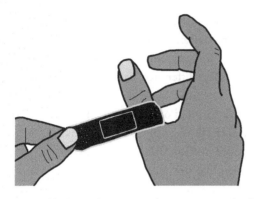

travel abroad, we might wonder how our particular stories may be alike or unlike other people's stories. While it's certainly sweet that my daughter found similarities between her skin color and the African American couple's at the choir show, our experiences as an economically privileged South Asian American immigrant family with many advantages might look and feel quite different than the lived experience of many Black people in the United States. Our skin colors might be similar but the historical and present manifestations of race and racism make our stories and lived realities quite different. As Ta-Nehisi Coates writes in *We Were Eight Years in Power*, "Racism is not merely a simplistic hatred. It is, more often, broad sympathy toward some and broader skepticism toward others. Black America ever lives under that skeptical eye." The particular history of anti-Black racism and continued racialization means that being Black in the contemporary United States is certainly different than being the kind of brown my family and I are.

These differences, too, are important to notice and speak aloud, to ask questions about, and to feel within our bones as well as see traces within our neighborhoods. We can ask: How might the history of slavery and the century of Jim Crow structural discrimination affect people's lives nowadays in the United States? How might the Indian Act of 1876 in Canada and other race-based policies affect present-day residential segregation patterns of First Nation and Indigenous people? How might these histories and policies—and the attitudes that accompany them—have implicitly and explicitly shaped the lives, opportunities, and professional trajectories of the African American couple from the choir show, the white elders enjoying the music, you and me, and so many others? Asking big questions helps us approach our complicated present better, less with *the* answer that will be the prized solution, but rather, with more humility. If we stay safe in silence and simply indulge our discomfort, we'll rarely speak frankly about our identities and experiences and about why those differences might matter in society, to whom, and in which contexts. We are, of course, living in a profoundly unequal world with too many difficulties for too many people. Let's speak aloud these issues, so we might also speak about what it might mean to shift these dynamics into something more humane and respectful for all.

Being Okay with Doses of Discomfort

Even with all my experience expanding my comfort zone and engaging with issues of identity and difference, I still did feel vexed when I watched others watching my daughter point out the Black couple at the choir show. I felt discomfort, yes, but tried to keep steady. I suppose in some ways, that's really the point: to be okay with the overwhelming feelings that we sometimes find ourselves with and not let those feelings take over the moment.

Oftentimes, our first reaction and response to feelings that make us uncomfortable is to want to change them, distract ourselves, or blunt the pain. How we approach topics and feelings that make us uncomfortable can tell us where we are tender, wounded, or raw. Guilt, shame, defensiveness, shutting down, denial, and other complex feelings keep us spinning within ourselves instead of looking up to be present, to better understand how we might untangle our own hurt and begin to interrupt unjust systems. It also prevents us from shining as brightly as we could. In our attempts to eradicate the tough emotions that we'd rather not feel, as researcher Brené Brown says, we also douse the positive ones. "You cannot selectively numb emotion.

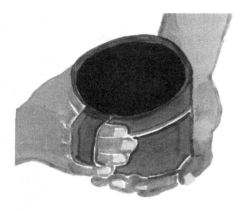

When we numb hard feelings, we numb joy, we numb gratitude, we numb happiness." What would it mean if we could soften our discomfort by being more curious about how our various emotions, thoughts, and stories sit in our bodies and play out in our interactions with one another? Might we even make friends with some of our uncomfortable feelings instead of rushing to extinguish them?

When we step into conversations about race and other differences, we address two things at once: the present and what's happening in front of us as well as the past and how we came to be where we are. It *is* overwhelming to learn about our history and how social structures were consciously designed to maximize profit and status for some people by keeping others down, especially if people who look like you benefited and continue to benefit from these policies and attitudes. We might feel guilty and bad—strong emotions that often breed silence, defensiveness, and shame. But staying silent and simmering in our guilt only fuels the unequal systems we want to dismantle. Instead, it would be so much more productive if we could step up and boldly notice what's around us and then use those uncomfortable moments as wake-up calls to better understand how we fit together in a much bigger, and yes, painfully unequal story.

A year or so after the gospel choir performance, I ran into the Black couple at a neighborhood shop. We recognized each other immediately. "Honey, look here!" the man had called out to his partner after shaking my hand. "It's the dancing kid's mom from the gospel show last year." He turned back to me. "That sure was a lovely afternoon. We had fun with your daughter. Please tell her that we, her 'brown friends,' say hi."

Stitched and Zipped: My Experience of Studying Abroad

Throughout my youth, my family and I had traveled to India from the United States every few years to visit our grandparents, cousins, aunties, uncles, and extended kin. My family are Indian immigrants, and I grew up in the United States. Though I had experienced these family trips to India as a child, as an undergraduate I wanted more—my own experience of learning and discovery. But my decision to study abroad in India seemed a strange choice for some of my classmates and teachers, one that signaled less a stretching of horizons and more a homecoming. "Why not go to France or Italy?" people asked me. "You already know things about India," they said. "Besides," they added, "won't it be easier studying in Europe?" I'm not opposed to Europe, but had never felt moved by the European stories, architecture, and famous sculptures that peppered the history books I read all through public school.

True, I did know some things about India, but compared to previous trips, this felt radically different. This long trip during college would be the first time I would go to India without my family, and to new areas of the country. In many ways, my story would be the familiar "child of immigrants returning to the homeland to find herself" journey, and I was both petrified and thrilled. My experience justified both these feelings.

Once there, even though my physical features helped me pass as a local—that is, until people heard my accent—I navigated the following eighteen months in India as a bit of an outsider, somewhat familiar, but still an outsider. This familiarity—however tenuous and fleeting—felt incredible to me, especially since I'd never felt like I properly belonged in the United States, despite having been born and raised in the country.

Throughout my youth, white children teased, taunted, and traumatized me for being brown and different. It started in preschool when kids made up a song about how I must have been dipped in chocolate milk. I vehemently protested, "I don't even like chocolate milk!" but did not understand why the song stung me so. In middle school, kids stuck gum in my hair, shoved me against lockers, and left me standing on the morning bus rides to school because no one gave me space to sit. I was called "curry girl," "backwards," and "too foreign to be American" (the last two by teachers), and repeatedly told that I had "looks that killed," based on the Mötley Crüe song that was popular back then. Though the song might have been written to celebrate the way someone looked, that's certainly not how it was being used to describe me. I hated being treated like this but didn't know how to explain the distress that felt almost physical. Like plumes of smoke, the racism I experienced stung my eyes and made my chest ache. It clung to me—hovering without being solid or named, and always clouding my vision. In response, I did what many of us who feel different and victimized do: I internalized the sadness and anger I felt and began to believe the loud noise from my surroundings that insisted I did not belong.

My coming-up-years, however, were also filled with goodness, warmth, and security. My wonderful parents created a safe and loving home, and we belonged to a community of friends—immigrants like us from the same region of India, who cherished us and made us feel seen. Good friends made me laugh, and I was busy all the time in school with choir, theater, and other activities. As a family, we enjoyed stability, safety, middle-class wealth, and we owned our own home. Going to India for a year and a half as an undergrad, then, pushed and pulled against my childhood experiences in important ways. Though parts of me had been torn apart by the racism of US culture, I found myself in India being nicely stitched back together. My time abroad helped me recognize layers of my family and culture, and know that where I came from mattered. Without the racist smoke of my youth burning my eyes and snaking up my nose, I started to see myself more clearly and breathe a bit deeper.

But the journey to and within India also unzipped my sense of self by making me question how authentically Indian I could ever be. I wasn't "really" Indian like the Indians around me; I was a privileged American entity mixed with migration and diaspora. Just as parts of me were now stitched back together, different parts of me had become unzipped. I wondered what and who was left of me?

Conversations That Didn't Happen

The actual university program under whose auspices I and the other fourteen students travel on does not provide much support to make sense of our daily experiences, nor our broader cultural stitchings or unzippings. Every few days, the program director makes a grand entrance through the carved wooden doors of the building the program rented in a posh area of town. "How are you all? Fine? Fine?" he thunders, not really waiting for an answer. He pays scant attention to what questions we harbor, how we are taught, what we learn, or even, really, how we fare. We are left mostly on our own with little leadership or accountability from faculty or program staff.

And so, my friends and I wander the dirt-road gullies of Old Delhi and the wide, paved thoroughfares of New Delhi with neither context nor connection. We are treated with curiosity and kindness from local people just as easily as we are swindled and duped. The rundown parts of the city that harbor refugee tents and makeshift tin dwellings feel different than the high-rise buildings that house the middle and upper classes. I don't know though, how to name or process the feelings that arise as I navigate the different neighborhoods. Why do I feel so awkward and guilty in the first setting, and awash with relief in the second? We do not talk about the big ideas that I and other classmates sift through—of class, poverty, being who we are in the world, noticing inequalities, and having more or having less than other people. Compared to the many local people we see and interact with, my classmates and I are all privileged Americans. Based on our particular identities, however, we are privileged and less-privileged in different ways. We aren't adept at initiating conversation on sensitive and weighty topics. Instead, we meander our way through the country uneasily, our questions and feelings about ourselves and the world silently simmering under the surface.

One of my classmates, who I'll call Ajay, is like me, an Indian American: family from India, he was raised in the United States. I think of him as somewhat unpredictable. Ajay isn't what you'd call "comfortable in his skin," and his hyphenated American-and-Indian identity seems to cause him great angst, especially now that he is smack dab in the motherland. I hear him continuously badmouth India to mollify his American self. "This place is so dirty," he says, "and smelly. And poor. It's disorganized. And too crowded." Sometimes he seems so sad and bitter. "I can't wait to go back home to a clean and civilized country. I'm so glad my parents fled this godforsaken land!" His anger—which seems more like shame at being forever associated with a place he had been told was considered soiled and crooked—preoccupies him continuously. Ajay's rants scare me, for while I too am figuring out how to be who I am between the United States and India, I don't want to be filled with negativity. I wonder to myself, should I act like him? Or might there be a less-condemning path to follow?

Another classmate I'll call Aaron spends the first few months of the program enthusiastic and bubbly. "Wow!" is his favorite go-to expression, applicable for all experiences. "Wow, the food!" "Wow, the women!" "Wow, the traffic!" "Wow, the colors!" During our class sessions on Indian civilization and society, taught by renowned Delhi University faculty, he always participates and asks insightful questions. Sometime midway in the year though, Aaron's enthusiasm peters out. He admits that being in India has unleashed a deep sense of historical remorse at not knowing enough about his own European immigrant roots. I remember him lamenting, "For twenty years I've been known as just a white guy in the United States. But all this history and culture here in India makes me want to have a history and culture too. My people must have had traditions and culture from our homeland, right?" He cries a lot those days, shoulders shrunken with sadness and regret. He eventually decides to leave the program to return home and initiate research about his white ethnic ancestry. Relinquishing a chunk of his program fees, within a few weeks, Aaron is back in the United States. A mutual friend tells me later that he returned a much heavier spirit, brooding and blue, quite changed from his earlier bubbly self.

Another classmate, a friendly and tall white woman I'll call Melody, finds herself the center of Indian male attention. According to her, wherever she goes young men stare at her with interest. She imagines that everyone wants to bed her. Some didn't, but I'm sure many did. She enjoys being pursued and wiggles her hips for her onlookers. "I'm always in the spotlight," she states, her finger twirling her shoulder-length hair. She giggles and tells us about her latest pick-up. The other students on our program and I listen to her sexy stories simultaneously incredulous at the attention she receives, and thoroughly jealous that we ourselves are clearly not so captivating. "The boys here are so nice to me," she says. And here she sighs. "Travel is wonderful. I love traveling. And I just looove Indian culture." As long as young Indian men ogle her, Melody enjoys India. When "the boys" do not give her the attention to which she's become accustomed, she falls into a terrible funk of culture shock, homesickness, and self-doubt.

I too am trying to make sense of my own identity. I spend much of my time quaking and hoping that people won't notice how  unsettled I feel. One night I go to a party with an incredible group of smart and worldly Delhi University students, where, haunted by all the times others have indicated, "you don't belong," I get caught up in my own head. I spend the evening an awkward wallflower, too nervous to speak and reveal the shame of being not-quite-Indian-enough and not-the-right-kind-of-American. Some version of this party dynamic repeats throughout my year and a half abroad: an excellent opportunity in front of me, and me plastered to the sidelines as the non-participant wallflower on account of the noise in my head that I do not know how to quell or quieten.

My time abroad also catalyzes numerous questions about what I observe and experience. Though I don't badmouth India too much like my classmate Ajay, I do wonder why India is so different than the United States. Public facilities like bathrooms in India are missing, or if present, scant and dirty. This contrasts greatly with the public facilities I have learned to take for granted in the United States. I knew a bit about the history of colonialism, but never quite grasped what made some countries rich and some countries poor. I ask myself if the lack of public amenities in India relates to a colonial past, or something else? How does this relate to the poverty, the tents, and tin shacks peppering the city? I think about Lakshmi, the daughter of my grandparents' domestic maid I knew as a child when I visited India, and feel guilty and bad. Lakshmi and I played together as children, though at some point, I learned to let her sweep and swab the rooms while I leisurely read comic books on the black vinyl sofa. How had I somewhat easily learned that she—along with her lower-caste identity, poorer social status, her labor—was there to support my upper-caste comfort? I see myself and my relative wealth implicated in the poverty all around me, but can't understand my feelings or what I am to do about it.

Likewise, I can't understand why Aaron feels bad about not knowing more about his white ancestry. The white children who tormented me throughout my youth seemed to get such a payoff from that very history. They felt they were better than me, and they proved it by their cocky attitude and unchecked behavior. Yet here was my good friend, sad and belittled because he doesn't know enough about himself and his ancestry. Is this the same phenomenon, or something different, I wonder.

I also think often about gender and sexuality during my time in India that year, about what it means to be a young woman in mostly male public space, and why I feel I have to cover my chest with scarves to seem modest and acceptable. I can't understand why I feel judgmental toward Melody's romantic liaisons. Everywhere we go together, she receives attention, and I do not. Is this because she is white? Or prettier than me? Both? Certainly, I feel inferior and envious. Perhaps, though, my feelings also have to do with the ways that her skin color marks her in different ways in India, but in seemingly better ways than my own skin color had marked me in the United States. Skin color is just skin color, I remember thinking. But no, some skin colors seem more desirable both in India and the United States. Why, I ask myself? Who made this so? How has it come to be that it is easier to be white both in the United States as well as in India? How does history inform our present in seemingly inescapable ways?

With no skills to speak aloud my questions and no formal classroom space to work them out, I try to be cool—liquid cool—and appear totally under control. To pull that off, I can't go very deep in conversations and need to stay on the surface of my emotions. My anxieties eventually do burst, like a pressure cooker gone rogue. I do not know how to be okay with the splattered mess of guilt and anxiety, so I panic and sprint out of my classmates' sight. Like a small animal in the presence of an approaching predator, I run this way and that, looking out for myself, fear and self-preservation coursing through my blood. I stay still, stay a wallflower, read a lot, and prefer to blend into the shrubbery than risk being seen.

Conversations That Can Happen

Nowadays, as I lead my own students abroad and consult with a range of programs, I feel heartbroken for the opportunities lost to us as a group so many years ago. It seems like such a shame that we had little scope to discuss any of the broader identity, difference, and power issues that clearly we all were struggling with, less to neatly solve them, and more to just acknowledge them as real. Perhaps I could have peeked out of my self-imposed refuge to participate in more conversations and experiences exactly as I was, not wishing I might magically change into someone else one lucky day. Among my peers I was often a wallflower but I did create a few friendships with local people, mostly people a generation older than me. These friendships allowed me a chance to bloom and grow. Among my peer group, though, I remained tentative without an outlet to process these feelings.

My peers also might have benefited from some honest and careful conversation about the issues they too seemed to be working through. I wonder if my Indian American classmate Ajay could have had a chance to reflect on the embarrassment he so clearly felt about being who he was if given the opportunity to explore what growing up different and brown in the United States in a sea of middle-class white meant to him. Perhaps he could have been guided to reflect on how that foundation shaped him, his shame of being himself, the costs of assimilation, and how he saw "the motherland" as flawed. In giving him opportunities to share and unburden, could we have perhaps lightened his load and ire toward his skin, his parents, and India itself?

I think about Aaron, whose lack of knowledge about his ancestry flooded him with a longing for a culture of his own. With some careful and sensitive talk, we could have spoken about the longer history of whiteness in the United States and the process through which immigrants from Europe and other light-skinned migrants were encouraged to leave behind their culture, assimilate, and become this-race-called-white. His not knowing his culture wasn't the fault of his family, but rather had to do with the broader history of immigration to the New World and how power was consolidated and deployed. I wonder what knowing this could have meant for his sense and search for self.

And for Melody, who felt that she was so warmly welcomed into the arms of Indian men, some frank talk about gender, sexuality, and race in an international context might have helped us all think about our identities in a more complex way. Though both Aaron and Melody were working through what being white abroad meant for each of them, Melody's journey as a white woman was gendered so differently than Aaron's as a white man. Perhaps we could have spoken about the troublesome associations related to white women abroad, that they are somehow emblematic of what is said to be the more developed and sexually liberated Western world, assumed to be available in a way that Indian women are assumed not to be. Of course, these were stereotypes, not applicable across the board. But if we had acknowledged and said aloud these underlying ideas—and made it less about us as individuals and more as an example of complex historical social phenomena—I wonder if all of us could have been supported to explore our feelings as white people and people of color abroad. We were all, of course, globally privileged women and men from what we were often told was "the best country in the world," in a majority brown country with strong patriarchal codes. And yet, we were finding, even within our small group, the different configurations that race made up when combined with gender and sexuality.

To spin these conversations constructively, we'd have needed trust, time, and tenacity as a group. We could have spared ourselves a great deal of angst if we had known that our emotional ups and downs weren't merely the result of our own flaws or shortcomings, but rather indicative of the complex global inequalities and geopolitical issues that many of us navigate when we travel. Like most programs peopled with Westerners who travel to the developing world, we did not have a faculty member, group leader, or program staff member who could facilitate the tricky and sensitive conversations we so desperately needed. On our own, we certainly did not know how to begin such honest talk. While we benefited greatly from the expertise of local Indian scholars who would guest-lecture our classes, we needed a person—or even a resource we could use—to help us think about issues of identity, race, culture, class, sexuality, and gender—and how

these concepts intersect with history, power, privilege, and justice. Knowing that we weren't alone in our thoughts could have helped us find more grace and empathy for each other, and certainly for ourselves. These conversations wouldn't have solved all our issues, but they would have helped us navigate our travels with less disconnect and more understanding.

Good Intentions and Do-Good Travel

Even now, more than twenty-five years since my classmates and I bumbled our way through our study abroad experience, most programs that send Westerners abroad rarely bring up—let alone honestly discuss—the kinds of identity experiences and emotional challenges that global travel sometimes glaringly brings to the surface. This matters greatly, for more young Westerners are venturing abroad than ever before. People from the West are meandering all over the planet to study, fix, heal, teach, build things, ally with and help others. In many ways, this makes good sense, as travel can broaden our horizons and provide perspective. There's really no other experience like hauling our body, head, and heart to another part of the planet to smell, taste, touch, hear, and see our amazing world. When we notice that some people might not have the same access and rights that other people take for granted, we may feel stirred to act. "I see that the world is unequal and too difficult for too many people," we may think, "and I want to help." Do-good travel hopes to catalyze well-intentioned sentiment into real-life solutions for the people who need them most. The many varieties of do-good travel include global health, medical missions, social impact cruises, development programs, alternative spring break, and voluntourism programs.

While there are differences in how each of these programs is conceptualized and run, most transport people of the Global North into resource-poor locations of the Global South. Sometimes, do-good travel can be aimed at resource-poor places in the Global North as well—for example, public health programs, service-learning opportunities, and educational pipeline programs. Some programs last a week or two, others for much longer. With such a variety of do-good travel opportunities from which to choose, the world as a destination is closer and easier to reach than ever before. Such programs are only growing in scope and number, offering more Westerners the chance to become "global citizens" and, as one advertisement puts it, to "see the world while making a difference."

Unfortunately, though, too many do-good travelers do not have the benefit of rich and critical conversations on many important issues, including the politics of our travels, how our identities give meaning to our lives, how our differences and similarities might resonate in a larger context, if good intentions are good for everyone, and what "help" means for whom in which context. As travel writer Bani Amor writes in their essay, "Getting Real about Decolonizing Travel Culture," thinking critically about travel of all kinds serves as "a vehicle for which to explore the condition of living, how our relationships to place shape us and our experiences, how our identities and political histories inform place, how power structures inform how we migrate (or don't) and how that affects the places we pass through." How we think of our journeys abroad matters greatly, as does our critical engagement with our home communities.

To approach our travel opportunities with critical awareness and reflection, we'll have to slow down our revved up desire to go and instead, first consider some big issues. We'll need to think more carefully about the broader ethics of identity, difference, and the global dynamics of power that have made it so that hundreds and thousands of Westerners jet-set around the globe to Ghana, Nicaragua, or Haiti to help, heal, and remedy what needs to be fixed, while hundreds and thousands of Ghanaians, Nicaraguans, or Haitians are similarly *not* coming to our countries to do the same. Rethinking travel in an unequal world gives us the tools to approach these big discussions with more humility and awareness. In the process, we strive to develop a more ethical and accountable backbone from which to act, both at home and abroad.

CHAPTER 2

Luggage We Take with Us:
Difference and Advantage

Differences Nearby

ACCORDING TO THE DIVERSITIES AND DISPARITIES PROJECT, MOST people in the United States live in residentially segregated communities that are not well integrated. The average white person, for example, continues to live in a neighborhood that is very different racially from those neighborhoods where the average Black, Hispanic, or Asian person lives. In metropolitan America, the average white person lives in a neighborhood that is 75 percent white. A typical African American lives in a neighborhood that is 65 percent Black, Hispanic and Asian and only 35 percent white. As these numbers suggest, just by living their lives in their own communities, true integration and diversity are experienced very differently in the daily lives of whites, Blacks, Hispanics, and Asians.

Given these realities, sometimes I speculate how it's even possible to know one another with deep honesty, trust, and openness across our identities and experiences. Though some of us *do* have meaningful relationships across race and income level, on the whole, we have few avenues to learn about one another in ways that do not already capitulate to the corrosive dynamics of power that structure our societies. It's no wonder we continue to be mired in stereotypes, misunderstandings, distrust, and discomfort when it comes to engaging in diversity and difference.

Preparing ourselves for our journeys abroad starts with developing the awareness and language to describe the differences in identities and experiences that are all around us even before we step onto the plane. Across the planet and even in our own communities, differences in life experiences, racial identities, and economic opportunities can bring to the surface uncomfortable feelings about, for example, who we are and how much we have compared to others. The material realities of these differences in advantages aren't just about our uncomfortable feelings. They play out in harsh and painful consequences for people, often based on who they are and the oppressive structures of our society. We can see this in the case of sexual assault against women and trans people because of misogyny and patriarchy, and with police surveillance and disproportionate violence toward Black people in the West because of racism, just to name two examples among many.

Our travels to culturally and economically different locations often turn into guilt trips precisely because we have little practice navigating the unequal power dynamics and different-than-me-ness we find. We're not always sure how to think or speak about the differences we notice, even though these differences might have fueled our desire to travel in the first place. Those of us with more privileges and social advantages, in particular, might be even less practiced in recognizing and saying aloud what it is we are noticing and feeling about identity, race, power, and hierarchy. Simmering in our guilt and discomforting feelings about systems we have not created but continue to participate in and perhaps benefit from does nothing for justice. Instead, we can build more comfort into talking about things many of us have been socialized not to. When we're less fragile and tripped up by our own discomfort, we build a better—and more authentic and lasting—foundation for global engagement.

In a journal devoted to international education, I read about a group of American private college students who visit a public high school civics class for an afternoon. The private college students will soon participate in a month-long study abroad program to Togo in West Africa. The visit to the high school class is the first of two visits the college students will conduct, one before the Togo trip and one afterwards. They've been sent by their French professor for two main reasons. One, to share their view that a second language can be the passport to see the world, and two, to ask the high schoolers what they want to know about West Africa so they can ask about it during their trip, and report back once they return. In this way, it's hoped that the college students' visits provide the high school students a window into opportunities beyond high school.

Though there are innumerable such programs that connect privileged college students with less-privileged high school students that strive to address the sizable resource, opportunity, and educational gaps between different communities, much less conversation exists on how these gaps might make us feel and how these interactions across difference might play out. I began to think about the dynamics of identity and advantage that might animate such interactions on both a social and personal level. And so, I created this story below based on the original journal article to see if I could explore how our guilt trips are less about the actual distance of the road traveled, and more about where the journey takes us.

Katherine and Ali: Next Door and Worlds Apart

The college students are all white, upper income and affluent, their youths spent in the suburbs lined with wide streets and green spaces. The students have enjoyed state-of-the-art facilities, dozens of unique extra-curricular afterschool classes from which to choose, and rigorous college-level offerings, all in their public schools outfitted like mini college campuses.

The high school students, by contrast, are mainly students of color, some Latino and mostly African American young people who live in an urban environment marked less by single-family homes and more apartment complexes. The high school interiors are illuminated with industrial bulbs rather than sunlight, and the building façade needs a paint job. Though many of the high school students assembled in the crowded classroom are earnest and hard-working, most have not had opportunities to take uncommon extra-curricular classes or travel out of state. Their working-class families cannot afford such extras. Most of the private college students, by contrast, have vacationed abroad. They see themselves as world travelers, their rich academic lives enhanced with winter trips to Aspen's ski resorts and summer backpacking trips through Western Europe.

The upcoming West Africa study abroad trip will not be the first time the college students have traveled to new places, but it represents something different than what they know. Traveling to Africa feels like a bigger cultural, racial, economic, and geographical leap than what they've been exposed to. It's a more momentous journey than many of their previous trips abroad, and they are collectively excited and quite a bit nervous.

The high school civics teacher, Mrs. Johnson, introduces the college students, and expresses how happy she is to have them visit her classroom—what a treat, what a great opportunity for her students. The college students glance at each other sheepishly. The fifteen-minute drive from their private college to the high school revealed manicured lawns in front of ivy-laced brick buildings quickly transform into corner liquor stores encased in metal grills. "Hope the car's still here when we return," they had laughed as they slammed the doors shut in the high school parking lot. They are the only white people in the room, and they are surprised at how different it feels to their eyes, heartbeat, and breath. Mrs. Johnson's effusive welcome has ended, and the students nervously begin the presentation about Togo and West Africa that they've rehearsed: Togo is here on the map. The official language is French. This is what Togolese people wear, this is what Togolese people eat.

Katherine, the college student leading this part of the presentation, has just finished telling the high school students how excited she is to improve her French in Togo. She asks brightly, "Any questions or comments?"

One of the high school students named Ali pipes up. "You all are going to Mother Africa? But Africa is *our* continent!" The class laughs, and Ali continues. "What are you all going to Africa for? Shouldn't you be going to France or England? *We* should be the ones going to Africa!" He's joking, kind of. He slaps the hand of his friend sitting next to him who has been murmuring affirmations of "That's right. You tell 'em."

Katherine starts to feel uncomfortable, although she isn't quite sure why. "Um, yes, we are going to Africa," she says to Ali. She wants to say more and respond to Ali's comment, but falters. She wonders if she should talk about the study abroad opportunities at her private college, those hundred-plus destinations from which she and her classmates have chosen the trip to Togo. Should she offer details about the program's theme of rural healthcare delivery, and her own interest in medical anthropology? Or maybe she should share her dilemma to choose either to go to Togo or a program in Australia focused on nursing. Togo eventually won out, for she and her family had already vacationed in Australia a few years back. Besides, going to Togo sounded more exotic. Katherine and most of her fellow student travelers don't know much about Africa. They know the tired stereotypes about universal poverty and corruption, of course, and are vaguely aware that there is more to the continent than what they've been exposed to. The students harbor great excitement about the opportunity to go somewhere so unfamiliar. Their trepidation, though, remains constant.

Katherine catches her mind drift, and decides to not say anything related to study abroad or travel. How many of the high school students in front of her will end up in a fancy private college like hers anyways? she thinks. A few? The majority? She considers how many Black and Latinx students she's seen on her college campus. The question gives her pause. Probably just a handful, she's surprised to realize. She is starting to recognize that she knows very little about urban high schools and students of color more generally. She abstractedly knows that the many opportunities she's had might not be akin to what Ali and his classmates have had access to. Standing in front of the high school class, the abstract ideas begin to take shape as real people with real lives. Guilt and shame now merge with her discomfort, but again, she's not quite sure why. Why is she feeling weird? Why *is* she going to Togo? Should she, as Ali suggested in his half-joke, half-real comment, actually be going to France instead? It would be more familiar to her, that's for sure.

Maybe in a few years Ali will go to a well-resourced college, she thinks hopefully, and sign up for his own study abroad program to Africa. Or will he? Katherine begins to realize that Ali's life pathway to adulthood as a young Black man might not be so neat and predictable as hers was as a young white woman from the suburbs. It's not like she can suddenly get Ali and his murmuring buddy to join them in Togo just because they as Black people have a historic link to Africa. Or wait: can she? Should she? She personally hasn't done anything wrong, but can't shake the fact that something, indeed, feels wrong in this moment. She looks around the room and feels the weight of her whiteness, wealth, and choices. Her face starts to tighten and redden, and she hands the microphone to one of her classmates. His eyes widen. He too is starting to look a bit woozy.

Global Citizenship

We are currently engaged in a broader public conversation about the educational value of travel to teach us about diversity and difference. In recent years, prominent people in education, as well as leading national figures, have championed global travel, and in particular, studying abroad, for all that it offers young adults. From community organization directors to presidents of US universities, preachers in suburban churches to high school principals, our leaders encourage us to go abroad, find and engage with difference, and return home global citizens. To be a "global citizen" means one enjoys popular esteem and regard these days. From what I've gathered, global citizenship will deliver for students any and sometimes all of the following:

- increased familiarity with diversity
- opportunity to learn how to interact with different people
- impetus to move out of one's comfort zone
- practice of valuable life skills such as experiencing new situations
- tools for future leaders to address critical issues
- challenges to confront inequality
- motivation to communicate with people of a different culture
- engagement with a multicultural world
- raised cultural competence
- preparedness to take on the global challenges of the 21st century
- encouragement to take risks

Global citizenship, then, is a catch-all phrase meant to describe a range of different priorities and skills meant to better individual students, and by extension, our societies. I've been curious about the term global citizenship for a while, and skeptical at its mammoth reach. I'd love for a well thought-out initiative to do all that it promises, from increasing students' understanding of diversity to encouraging young people to take on global challenges. Can it, though? I wonder: can travel to places unlike what one knows, and interaction with new kinds of people different from who we usually know, really fulfill our hopes for a generation? Study abroad and other models of educational and experiential programs send students away to Togo and any number of countries to grapple with difference—coded as diversity—with the hopes of becoming global citizens. Racial, economic, and cultural differences, though, are often much closer at hand; one need not travel twelve thousand miles. Sometimes, as Katherine and the other private college students learned, a mere twelve miles will do just fine. Perhaps what differences we expect to find abroad—and what we might learn from that—depends less on how far one travels, and more on who we are, what we've been exposed to, and the diversity or homogeneity of our home communities.

Exposure to Difference and Diversity

For people who have grown up in culturally insular communities, like these nine private college students, any kind of travel—even local travel across town to a new neighborhood twelve miles away—can be jarring, meaningful, and instructive. The college students had assumed that going to Togo would be an intense experience, an experience that would make them stretch from what they knew. They had not considered this two-hour high school visit would also stretch them. Never before had these nine white college students interacted with so many students of color at one time and in one place. Never before had they been asked to consider what it might mean for them to go to Togo based on who they were in the world. This high school clocked a mere twelve miles away from their elite college, and yet temporarily opened up a world of racial, cultural, and economic difference even before they boarded their flight to Africa. What? they thought. So much intensity and stretch already, so close to home? They encountered lived realities that looked quite different than what they personally knew. This example, focused around domestic difference, can help us understand what kinds of difference and diversity we might be exposed to—and which social issues might be salient—closer to home as well. In this way, we can begin connecting our local environments to the broader global issues we might be learning about.

Looking at this story, we may find it surprising, but not unusual, for a group of affluent white private college students to never have spent time in a room of mostly Latino and Black students. We may also find it surprising, but not unusual, for a group of Latino and Black students from working-class families to never have spent time with a group of white students from affluent families in this way too. In the West, many of our residential, educational, professional, and social worlds rehearse long-standing patterns of racial and economic segregation, carving out spaces where we live, learn, work, and play in contexts where predominantly everyone looks like us and reflects our own culture and norms.

What Do We Do with Differences?

Difference is an odd thing; sometimes, we fear it; other times we want it. In our culture of "be like me," difference stands out. Difference can be thought of as an irritant or flaw, making those of us who are different (in a variety of ways) more visible, scrutinized, sized up, and disciplined. In other ways, though, difference draws us in. It sparkles and shimmers with novelty, making those of us who are different (again, in a variety of ways) more visible, and sometimes, more alluring. In the first case, dif-

ference becomes the repository of our fears; in the second, the repository of our desires. Sometimes, our contradictory fear or desire of difference even takes root within the same moment. When we slow down and notice our thoughts and feelings about difference, we realize what an enigma it is. We look for difference, crave it, curiously approach it, and sometimes, recoil and crush it. Ambivalent at best, we aren't always sure how to categorize it.

Travel abroad draws upon and complicates our fear of and desire for difference. So many of us make journeys to far-away lands, specifically searching for something different than what we know. We hope to find cultures, people, ways of life, stories, experiences, foods, sights, and geographies that will be novel and fresh. As travelers, we seek difference and pay a premium to ensure we will find it. We hope for "real and authentic" experiences, and we revel in the unfamiliarity.

What else do we "do" with difference once we've found it?

We consume difference,
flirt with difference,
and sometimes,
assimilate and discipline difference into something
not-so-different.
We ogle and worry over,
and are attracted to and avoid difference.
We photograph and frame,
tag and like difference.
We obsess about difference,
eroticize and bed difference.
We commodify and celebrate difference
(as long as that difference doesn't
    marry our daughters
    buy homes near ours
    or challenge our power).

We eat and drink difference, yum!
We worry we will offend difference, yikes!
And so we
    tiptoe,
    whisper,
    eggshell and
    hedge around different kinds of difference.
We tread gingerly around our guilt,
careful not to wake that
    snoozing monster of a giant,
    light-sleeper that he is.
We feel special and accomplished
once we've traversed difference.
And sometimes, even though our travels take us higher and higher,
farther and farther away from home,
we aren't quite sure which
                way
                    is
                       up.

Noticing and Naming

Paying attention to our different identities invites us to talk together and better understand the broader social dynamics of which we are a part. We know that society systemically gives advantages to some identities and makes life more difficult for others. Our interactions with each other are often born from how we've been socialized to understand ourselves and others, as well as the larger social contexts we've been raised in. These facts compel me to intentionally observe what is around me. I can't fix everything or remedy all the ills of the world, but if I pay close attention to details, patterns, and behaviors associated with identity and social advantage, I can better understand how power dynamics work, how they are reproduced consciously and unconsciously, and how I might be more effective in interrupting the unjust structures around me. I often ask myself the following set of noticing and naming questions:

- Who is present and who is not?
- How many of this kind of person are there, how many are not? Why might that be?
- Whose voice is heard most, what kind of person is more visible, and why?
- Whose voice is less heard, silenced, or missing from the conversation, and why?
- Whose image is reflected back at us more often than others, and whose image is invisibilized?
- What stories get top billing or don't, and why?

Noticing and naming our surroundings can be a powerful way to focus in on differences in our identities and what these differences might mean. We can use these questions to reflect on a range of different fields and arenas. Media representations are a good illustration of where such questions can illuminate the status quo power structures, and what feels wrong or threatening or strange or all of these if we change things up. We can ask: which kind of actor gets cast for what role and what does that mean for different kinds of people? Let's say we're looking at a fairly typical situation where a white actor is cast as an Asian character. Could the same thing happen if we replace the races and have, say, an Asian actor cast as a white character? Are these situations the same thing, or something altogether different? Another example: if Katherine and her fellow private college students in the earlier story had visited a well-funded, suburban, mostly white high school similar to the ones they had attended, would they have questioned their place in the classroom, all that they have had access to, and their upcoming visit to Togo in the same way? Though we might not know the answer to the questions we ask, the questions are critical to consider. In so doing, questions like these help us better understand what's happening both in front of us and behind the scenes. When we learn to notice what is around us, we are able to see both ourselves and our context beyond the surface from different angles and viewpoints.

Personal Learnings

As I've learned to intentionally observe my surroundings, I've also become more aware of how I am feeling in different situations. Paying attention has helped me better understand the discomfort I often experience when it comes to crossing differences in race, gender, sexuality, poverty and wealth, disability and opportunity. I spent a long time pretending I didn't notice what I saw all around me because I didn't know how to handle the feelings arising from what I saw. I felt horrible and confused at the injustices and the inequality I noticed in my community or read about. While I certainly yearned for change, I didn't realize my own complex feelings of guilt, shame, and incomprehension were also part of the picture. And so, I dimmed my eyes from the uncomfortable sights I saw and soaked in my own negativity.

These days, I'd rather put my energies into noticing what's around me and staying present. I am learning and practicing how to shift the self-sabotaging feelings into something more productive and justice-oriented. I've learned that if I stay too focused on my own unprocessed feelings, I'm not so useful or receptive to others. Instead, I'd rather try to be open and pay attention to what is in front of me without the constant chatter of insecurity, doubt, guilt, and shame ringing in my ears. I'd rather be centered and open to my feelings instead of having them rule me. In this respect, I've learned a lot from rehearsing the set of naming and noticing questions listed earlier, and by watching how other people notice and navigate their surroundings. Paying attention to what other people notice (or not notice) has helped me develop my own observational skills.

Holding Space

In my racial equity consulting as well as my university work, I often hear people say how nervous they are to share their questions, vulnerabilities, and difficult experiences about difference, identity, and the feelings these topics inspire. They're nervous to share with people in general, and even more so with people they perceive are "not like them." We worry: What will people think of me if they know I'm confused, overwhelmed, or not always right and in control? How will I be perceived based on who I'm around? For those of us in the minority, sharing with people "not like us" takes on another layer: Can I share hard things, especially if I'm one of few people of color in the group, if I'm the only immigrant, if I'm the only openly gay person? As you read through the stories in *Beyond Guilt Trips*, you will recognize where all of these issues were unconsciously happening for characters featured in the narratives. Often that person is me.

Some of this makes good sense. Being honest about ourselves and our experiences often requires a foundation of trust and comradery, a sense that what we share will be valued and understood. And though when we're abroad in a group we often forge tight bonds quickly, trusting one another with our vulnerabilities is doubly or triply tricky when it comes to conversations on race in mixed company. Sharing our personal experiences across identities and especially across race feels more difficult, risky, and vexed than sharing experiences with others who might be more "like us."

The difficulty we feel is not a surprise. Our difficulty is evidence of the long history and present manifestations of institutional racism; racism's connections to gender, sexuality, class, and other social categories; residential patterns of segregation; the culture of miseducation; and little exposure to different kinds of people in meaningful ways. Our conversations become stilted and skewed because most of us have had little opportunity to socialize and share with different kinds of people in repeated, low-stakes everyday moments. The low-stakes and everyday part of this is key. Many of the people I work with say that because they've had so little practice in cross-racial spaces, when an opportunity does present itself to share or talk together the moment becomes "overdetermined," that is, the moment has to do everything because *this is it*! Overdetermined moments suffer from too much expectation without the social structures for back up. Consequently, when we need to talk about racial categories, how we're differently positioned, and how all this makes us feel, we're not sure what to expect or even how to begin. We worry about how it might go, we steep in discomfort, and we anticipate the worst.

Part of my work is to chip away at overdetermined and high-stakes one-off conversations that must do everything and, instead, create more spaces where different kinds of people can practice conversations about tough or tricky issues more often. Like reps at the gym, practicing helps us build capacity and stretch, and doing this often helps to familiarize ourselves with the uncomfortable feelings that might come up. When we normalize the uncomfortable sensations and know that they will pass and we'll be okay, we're able to engage and not shut down. I've witnessed transformative shifts in people's engagement with sensitive issues when they're able to practice sharing and listening deeply across different identities in more regular and low-stakes ways. Listening to others deeply is a process, and is often called "holding space" for another. Holding space invites us to be fully present with the people in front of us, to listen or participate without instantly wanting to fix, and to hear without always interjecting our solution. Holding space for others also means noticing what's coming up for us—what kinds of thoughts or doubts or anxieties might arise—so we are then able to attend to ourselves and others with compassion, less judgement, and kindhearted curiosity.

- -

Holding Space Together

The following questions—and throughout in the "Holding Space Together" sections—are designed to open up ways to relate to and engage with the stories and ideas I set out in this book. They are questions I've used in my own life and use in my workshops. Some of the questions encourage us to slow down, to see things from another angle, or make connections with what others have said and thought. Take some time with these sections, for most of us haven't grown up learning how to discuss the issues raised in this book. These prompts work well in a group—

friends, classmates, colleagues, or the people you're traveling with—and help us think together and practice how to talk with one another.

You might want to start a notebook or journal to respond to the questions and prompts, free-writing your way to deeper reflection and insight. These prompts aren't about a right or wrong answer—there rarely is one when it comes to issues of identity, difference, and the various feelings these concepts inspire. I've found these prompts to be useful, for myself and others, as a way to be more inquisitive about who we are in the world, how our ideas have been shaped over the years, and where we'd like to go from here.

- Think back to the story I told in chapter 1 of my daughter at the gospel choir show and to when you were young. What do you remember noticing about identities and differences, race and hierarchy, advantage and disadvantage? Did you grow up in a household in which you said aloud what you noticed and thought, or not? How might this upbringing have affected how you now notice or do not notice what's around you?

- Consider a moment when your own desire for safe politeness made you say or do certain things. How did it feel at the time? What kinds of stories were circulating in your mind about what might happen if you said aloud what you really thought?

- As you consider your own comfort with emotions and logic, how might you practice bringing together your thinking heart *and* feeling head space? If we're not used to "thinking with our heart" and "feeling with our mind," it can be difficult to bring together the head and heart spaces. Logic and a focus on facts and rationality can easily feel more convenient and familiar than holistically combining our emotions and logic while moving through the intense feelings that identity, belonging, and inequality often raise. As my friend Sasha Duttchoudhury writes, "It takes a different kind of boldness to know answers through the gut than from the mind when the mind doesn't want to see what is really there. It must take a genius of the heart to know these truths, and to be patient enough with others to help them grow into this truth."

- How does encountering difference and thinking about justice help you trace, as scholar Michelle Liu says, the "changing tides in empathy within oneself for others? What emotions are swept in, and what emotions swept out"? When can these tidal sweeps be helpful? When not?

- Next time you find yourself in moments of discomfort, how might you make use of the strategy of slowing down to notice how you feel and what is around you?

- -

The Mythical Norm: Closer to Power and Further from Awareness

In the story at the beginning of this chapter, Katherine the college student felt uncomfortable with high schooler Ali's comments in the classroom for many reasons. As a white person, she hasn't had to think too much about race, and consequently, isn't so practiced in noticing how it works. This isn't because Katherine is particularly obtuse, but rather reflects how each of us notices or doesn't notice things based on our identities. We are, of course, treated differently based on our lived experiences of what we look like, which groups we belong to, and how those groups are categorized and ranked in society. Our identities—Katherine being white or you being Black or he being queer or me being a woman—are never just empty facts. The layers of social meaning and the ways that power manifests through racism, patriarchy, and homophobia make the facts of these identities matter in a larger world.

In each society, the group of people who are seen as somehow better than others are considered the norm against which other identities are judged and viewed. This is true in our home communities as well as when we travel abroad. As Audre Lorde writes in her book *Sister Outsider*: "Somewhere, on the edge of consciousness, there is what I call a mythical norm, which each one of us within our hearts knows 'that is not me.' In the West, this norm is usually defined as white, thin, male, young, heterosexual, Christian, and financially secure. It is with this mythical norm that the trappings of power reside within this society." Identities and experiences that are closer to the mythical norm reflect closer proximity to the seat of symbolic power, attractiveness, and desire. Privilege can look like being male in a male-dominated society and being white in a culturally dominant white society. The more identities we have that are closer to the mythic norm, the more benefits one receives. And the more benefits one receives—like Katherine and her classmates' whiteness and wealth and access to resources—the less we've probably had to consider how that particular issue affects our lives. Additionally, the closer we are to the mythical norms, the more we might unconsciously and unwittingly police societal boundaries to maintain power and ensure the status quo will benefit us. We might be nervous to recognize our benefits and privileges for fear they might be diminished or altogether taken away. This, too, contributes to the silence, discomfort, and defensiveness that often accompanies such conversations.

If privilege refers to how close you are to Lorde's mythical norm, oppression refers to how far you are from the center and how this marginality manifests in your life. Distance from the mythical norm can exhibit itself as marginalization, violence, disenfranchisement, and struggle that some people experience at the hands of more privileged people, all because they are somehow different than those who have more power. The further we are from the center of power, the more conscious we often are of the mythical norm, and the more we might agitate for change.

More or Less Visible

In her book *Why Are All the Black Kids Sitting Together in the Cafeteria? And Other Conversations on Race,* Beverly Daniels Tatem gives us strategies to understand how different experiences can be more or less visible to us based on our context. She points out that while many see a group of Black (or Asian or Latino) kids sitting together in a school cafeteria, we often don't see the groupings of white students in the same way. Tatem helps us understand why one group is more visible than the rest, and how the Black kids' hyper-visibility intimately connects to the white kids' under-the-radar regular-ness. She writes, "If individuals are members of a dominant or advantaged group, they take their identity for granted. Conversely, if not, then they're made very conscious of their identity because others take notice, especially since they are considered different from the norm."

This concept of hyper-visibility and under-visibility takes place often in my everyday life. Just recently, a white acquaintance mentioned to me how excited she was that an event we had attended was "so diverse." Diversity, of course, means different things, but in this case I knew the person was talking about racial diversity. I was momentarily taken aback at this assessment of the event being "so diverse," for, at first glance, in an audience of about seventy white people it looked like there was only me and another three people of color. Four individuals of color in a group of seventy people works out mathematically to 5.7 percent racial diversity, which to me, isn't very diverse at all. It shouldn't be considered particularly diverse to anyone, actually. And yet, to my acquaintance, the normality and default position of her own whiteness made the 94.3 percent of whites in the room under-visible, and the 5.7 percent diversity represented by the people of color in the room seem hyper-visible. We four people of color stood out and were visually pronounced based on her limited awareness of the power of the status quo to define our reality and gaze.

When You Feel Ordinary and When You Can't

Like my diversity-observing acquaintance, many white people in majority white contexts feel "ordinary" and "regular," not because they are particularly insensitive or dense, but because their racial identity is the norm that is all around and they haven't had to question this fact. This is an important point also when we're abroad. In the next chapter we'll hear from many white travelers about how the fact of being white abroad felt much less "ordinary and regular," something they hadn't even realized they were used to at home. Much of the Western media—such as movies, television, books, and advertisements, as well as the mainstream curriculum in most schools—upholds and reflects whiteness as that which is everywhere, and we rarely ask critical questions to help us notice and name our surroundings. This means we can remain quite unaware of how power structures operate, even if our good intentions might compel us otherwise.

So normalized is whiteness in most Western contexts that many white people feel that they don't even have a race. "I'm not really anything," a twenty-year-old white college student named Mike admits in a workshop I'm facilitating about race. "I'm just a regular American." Like many white people, Mike is unaccustomed to talking about race. He flounders to find his words, but bravely presses on and practices sharing. "I don't think I'm like some of the other people in this room. I don't have a race like the Asian or Black people do. I'm not sure how to even contribute to a conversation on race if I don't have one."

In the same workshop, Jayla, a twenty-one-year-old Black woman, sighs deeply and responds. "Growing up in a mostly white neighborhood, I've always had to know two things: that I was Black, and that I was not white. It's frustrating to know that my experiences are so different than many of the white people here." Jayla gathers her thoughts. She's poised and sensitive, and generous in sharing her experiences with the group. She continues, "There hasn't been a single day that I haven't thought of the fact that I am Black and not white. I'm not saying that it's always bad to be me. I love who I am and what I am. I'm just saying that I have always had to think of my race, every single day. White people of course have a race, but don't have to think about it all that much."

Jayla clearly understood long ago the difference her skin color made to her life. Mike, however, had been protected by the privileges of being, in this case, closer to the mythic norm. He has had little occasion or necessity to think through his whiteness the way Jayla has had to think about her Blackness. The closer we are to the mythic norm of society, the more difficult it is to always see the connections between our own lives and the broader institutions that structure them. As white anti-racist educator Peggy McIntosh writes in her now-famous essay "Unpacking the Knapsack": "I was taught to see racism only in individual acts of meanness, not in invisible systems conferring dominance on my group." For many white people, racism is about individual prejudice. For people of color, however, racism is often systemic, institutionalized, and structural. When it comes to race, Mike and Jayla, Katherine, Ali, the Black couple who played with my child at the concert, and you or me for that matter, all enter the conversation from different points of view and privileges that have made us acutely aware of some things and less aware of other things.

These gaps in our perception sometimes make talking across difference extremely challenging. "How can you not notice what I notice?" we might think. "It's so obvious to me. But for you, privilege means it hasn't had to be."

The structures of inequality and their impact on so many people's lives is indeed infuriating. A better understanding of mythical norms and normalized privilege can help encourage conversations about racial equity and other issues with less resentment and more equanimity, less blame and more openness. It is hard to notice things you haven't had to see because your privileges have shielded you from having to notice. You can't blame people for not knowing what they don't know. When people begin to open their eyes and ears to different stories and start to realize how power relations are not only individualized but structural, that's when we see big growth and opportunities for justice work.

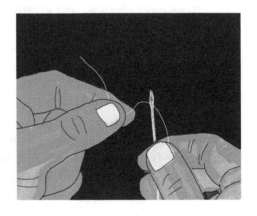

It's essential to say that this kind of critical thinking process and learning isn't always comfortable or easy. Acknowledging the benefits of our positionality based on the mythical norm can be challenging to admit and hurtful to process. We'd rather believe that our wins and successes solely stem from our hard work and individual determination rather than power structures that have given us numerous tailwinds and invisible leg-ups. If we can stay curious and stay away from defensiveness, we'll better understand what else we might have been shielded from and how that benefits the status quo. Staying curious and present also helps us understand how oppressive structures for marginalized people in society actually contribute to the woundedness of all of us.

Attending to this can be a healing move. When we begin to consider how our identities might have affected our way of seeing the world and interpreting life around us, we take an important step forward.

Intersectionality: When We're Many Things at Once

While it is true that white people are closer to the mythical norm when we are talking about race, it's also true that each of us inhabits many more identities and experiences in addition to our race. Take the college student Katherine. Yes, Katherine is white and comes from a wealthy family with incredible amounts of cultural capital. All that matters. So, too, does the fact that she is one of three women in her mechanical engineering class and feels that she has to work twice as hard as her male classmates for half the credit. So too does the fact that though she's heard about female empowerment and how "women can do anything" her whole life, fear of sexual assault makes her too nervous to walk home from the campus library late at night if she's by herself. These experiences of being a woman in a patriarchal society play out in Katherine's life, and complicate her position in society. When we layer all of Katherine's identities—or mine or yours—it's clear we're now looking at a more intricate picture of how close or far one might be to the mythical norm than if we were viewing ourselves from only one identity.

That we hold many identities and experiences at once is what we refer to as intersectionality, a term coined by Black feminist legal scholar Kimberle Crenshaw. All of us are many identities at once, and each of these identities interacts with the rest. Some identities, to reference Jeanette Winterson's novel, are "written on the body," that is, visible and obvious to others. Some identities are invisible and unknown to others unless shared. Though we often notice the one or two most clearly present and visual differences in each other—race and gender, usually—all of us are intersectional in ways we can see and not see.

For people whose identities are closer to the mythical norm, there's often a big learning curve associated with noticing the invisible systems that bestow power on our own group. We might feel uncomfortable, guilty, or bad the more we look around, name what is happening, ask questions, notice how power works, and understand what that means for people's lived realities. Mike and Katherine both are learning about what being white means in a world structured by powerful racial categories, though they are learning about it from different gendered experiences. Mike is navigating his life as a young white man, Katherine as a young white woman. Mike is yes, white and male, and also someone whose father is deaf and who is a first-generation college student. These identities and experiences compound together to make Mike who he is in the world—and Katherine and Ali and you and me—whether we can "see" evidence of all these experiences or not.

In his book *Exile and Pride: Disability, Queerness and Liberation,* Eli Clare poignantly describes his experience of intersectionality in this way: "Gender reaches into disability; disability wraps around class; class strains against abuse; abuse snarls into sexuality; sexuality folds on top of race . . . everything finally piling into a single human body. To write about any aspect of identity, any aspect of the body, means writing about this entire maze. This I know, and yet the question remains: where to start? . . . There are a million ways to start, but how do I reach beneath the skin?"

When we hold space for ourselves and our discomforting feelings—when we reach beneath the skin of our own biases, miseducation, and hurts—we begin the process of racial healing on our own and with others. As Debby Irving writes in her book *Waking Up White, And Finding Myself in the Story of Race,* "If there's a place for tolerance in racial healing, perhaps it has to do with tolerating my own feelings of discomfort that arise when a person, of any color, expresses emotion not welcome in the culture of niceness. It also has to do with tolerating my own feelings of shame, humiliation, regret, anger, and fear so I can engage, not run. For me, tolerance is not about others, it's about accepting my own uncomfortable emotions as I adjust to a changing view of myself as imperfect and vulnerable. As human."

Am I saying that if you're closer to the mythical norm with invisible advantages you will be perpetually happy and content in your smooth sailing life? No, I am not. Am I also saying that people who experience marginalization or fewer advantages are doomed to lead a pathetic life of gloomy deprivation? Certainly not. But are there measurable opportunities some of us have access to that others do not based on a history of inequality and the perpetuation of a status quo that provides more things for fewer of us? Most definitely, yes.

In chapter 1, I mentioned that I was treated horribly by some white classmates and teachers because of my race. This was, of course, a disadvantage or oppression related to my distance from the mythical norm of being white, and an example of how racism, nativism, and discrimination played out in my youth. At the time, though, I never really thought about all the advantages or privileges I simultaneously benefited from during those same years: my family's documented citizenship status; my father's professional class job that provided stability and a regular salary, enough food to never know hunger, enough wealth to purchase our own home and take modest vacations; a strong cultural focus on education; and so much more. Earlier, I never considered these advantages because I never really had to deal with their lack or distance from the more privileged norm. Later, though, I began to examine my life from multiple angles and ask more questions about why things were the way they were. I realized that I had more stability, wealth, health, and opportunity than many others in my community and around the world, and had very little language beside a soupy guilt to explain my complex feelings. These advantages did not, of course, diminish the sting of racism that I experienced or how I, even now, continue to experience being a dark brown woman of color in a default white society. My numerous advantages did and do, however, make my life that much easier than if I and my family had been dealing with other serious issues as well.

Because many of us in the West have systemic resources and advantages from which to draw from, we'll have to work harder to see what has been invisibilized to us. None of us are outside of this system. As James Baldwin famously wrote, "Nobody is more dangerous than he who imagines himself pure in heart; for his purity, by definition, is unassailable." The more we consider these issues from an empowered standpoint, the more we can stay with our feelings. That's the only way we'll be able to transform our guilt trips into relationships based on affinity, understanding, and connection.

- -

Holding Space Together

- Think about the people around you: friends, family, neighbors, classmates, colleagues, and wider community. Do most of the people around you look like you? When did you first become aware of who is around you and why that might be so?
- How often do you talk about race, identity, or culture with your friends or family? Why do you think that is so? How do you think your identities have encouraged you to notice or not notice certain things about power, privilege, history, and society?
- How close to or far away from the mythical norm would you define yourself based on race? What about gender, class, access

to resources, religion, education, mobility, and other factors and identities? You might want to experiment with art to explore how your myriad identities and experiences relate to the mythical norm. You can create a chart, illustrate interlocking concentric circles, or try out any number of images and visual representations.

- How would you describe your own intersectional identity and experience of being you? Feel free to experiment with different kinds of prose, as creative writing can help us practice thinking outside the boxes we're most often in. You might want to emulate Eli Clare's "experience of intersectionality" paragraph with your own personal configuration of what makes you reach beneath your own skin.

- Think about sharing an afternoon over a pot of tea with someone of a different identity or life experience than you. How comfortable would you be talking about the thing-that's-different between you two? Consider how our comfort or discomfort might be associated with the ways we've been raised, the contexts we've inhabited, the conversations we've had or not about sensitive social issues, identities, difference, and power.

- Have you experienced feeling the soupy guilt I describe? What did it feel like to you? Where do you think this feeling comes from? What do you think it takes to transform this disempowering feeling into something less individual, less shameful, and more collective?

CHAPTER 3

- -

Ticket Bought, Part One:
Identity, Culture, and Race

WE STUFF OUR BAGS AND KISS OUR FRIENDS AND FAMILY GOODBYE. Suddenly, we've arrived in Ghana, Tanzania, or Honduras with curiosity and good intentions: here we are! Before we know it, though, our emotions can go through the wringer. As travelers we may feel warm and triumphant one moment, or frustrated and close to breaking the next. Sometimes our frustrations stem from concrete mishaps like our missed bus or our leaky gut. Less concrete, and perhaps just as confounding, are the ways our identities take on different meanings abroad. Some identity of ours that might have seemed ordinary or unnoticeable at home—our hair, skin, or access to opportunities— seems unique or special in this new context, and local people respond in kind. Vendors might circle us wherever we go. Children might follow us. "Your skin, your hair!" someone might call out as they touch our different-than-their-own skin or hair. Maybe it's our whiteness or Blackness or Asianness that's suddenly on display. Or maybe, because we've come from a wealthy country, local people imagine our pockets to be cascading with cash. Sometimes, though, parts of who we are might seem unrecognizable or untranslatable in the new context we are in. Our journeys to different lands can make us reflect on the different ways we are always "me," and also somehow not.

Friendly Vendors and Prickly Feelings: Identity, Culture, and Race

Many years ago, I toured Morocco with a group of US educators for six weeks on a program explicitly focused on Islam, gender, and crossing cultural boundaries. This is a mere few years after September 11, 2001, and right in the middle of the long retaliatory war in Afghanistan. My fellow educators and I want to learn from Moroccans about, yes, their religion, but also about the challenges and joys people feel in their own communities as they go to work, raise families, celebrate festivals, and deal with the flow and flux of life. We are committed to better understanding this region of the world, and happily we set out to learn.

Within a day or two after our arrival, my colleague Ahmed and I notice that we attract attention in a particular way, different from the rest of the group. He and I are the two people of color in our large group of otherwise eighteen white Americans. When we enter any kind of tourist zone, from an important shrine in Rabat to the wide open-air markets in Marrakesh, local vendors rush to the white participants to advertise their goods and make a sale. Vendors also rush to Ahmed and me, less to sell their wares, though, and more to guess where we are from. "Pakistan?" people ask me repeatedly. "Sri Lanka?" "Ethiopia?" "Libya?" "India?" Ahmed also elicits his own catalogue of countries from where he might hail. "Somalia?" "Kenya?" people surmise. "Ghana?" "South Africa?" The friendly hubbub around our skin color and ethnic origins continues in whichever part of the country we travel.

Fellow program participants also notice the way Ahmed and I are treated. A few of us laugh together about the funny and sometimes awkward interactions. And it takes me a little while to get used to it. In the United States, "Where are you from?" is often a loaded question, depending on who's asking it and in what context. When white people ask other white people the question, they're often asking a geographical question: where were you before you came here, which state or region are you from? In my experience, though, when a white person asks a person of color this question, it can feel different. The question might be a small-talk conversation starter for the questioner, but for the immigrant, person of color, or "unrecognizable" accented recipient, the question sometimes feels like an unconscious path for the white person asking to figure out where your brown skin is from or why you talk the way you do. It's a way to quickly identify the difference in you and be able to manage it with a category: "Oh, you're from India or Thailand or mixed-race Cambodian and Black or third generation Chinese American. Ah yes. Now I see. Now I can make sense of you." The questioner may not have meant anything by the interaction, but the longer history of whiteness, racialization of people of color, and the incessant questioning of our belonging in both small and big ways makes the impact of the question sometimes more important or urgent than the questioner's intent.

In Morocco, though, the vendors' insistence on finding out where we are from feels quite different to me. I begin to realize that the context in which I had been asked that question hundreds of times before has shifted, and that here, I feel and respond differently. I relax into the interactions, enjoy the laughter, and appreciate the chance to chat with vendors and shopkeepers one on one. Ahmed and I both use the attention received from our different-than-our-traveling-group skin color as a way to practice our beginning Arabic and deepen our understanding of local culture.

The "Sri Lanka? Ethiopia? Somalia?" hubbub, though, begins to elicit ambivalence in a good number of our group members. Ahmed and I notice that if a Moroccan comes up to us to guess our origins, a few colleagues sigh, roll their eyes, or turn their head away. They slide their focus toward a colorful shawl or a pair of embroidered leather slippers on display in a roadside shop, anywhere but where the Moroccans are commenting on our skin color and cultural origins. At the time, I'm not sure how to read my colleagues' ambivalence.

Maybe my colleagues think that the Moroccans who ask about our origins are racist or inappropriate. Perhaps they feel that Ahmed and I are being treated unfairly special and become resentful. Maybe my colleagues themselves are having a tough time being a foreigner and displace their anxieties onto us. And maybe for a few of them, there is just nothing to say, especially when you'd rather be left alone to shop for embroidered leather slippers. Increasingly, though, I get the feeling that something tetchy about identity and cultural and racial discomfort is taking place—something that is beyond the attention that Ahmed and I receive but related. The "Sri Lanka? Somalia?" moments take on an energy of their own, the sighs, eye rolls, and bad vibes of some group members only increase, and I continue to feel both a part of and outside of my traveling group.

Some group members conduct themselves with equanimity and ease. But some colleagues become more troubled by the cross-cultural interactions and find themselves acting in ways they might not have imagined for themselves. One afternoon a few weeks into our travels, a group of vendors approach our group with the familiar intention of showing us carpets. Most of the vendors we have met haven't been overtly pushy, and if someone isn't interested in purchasing their wares a shake of the head and a smile is generally enough to continue our journey. We are, to be sure, a highly conspicuous group of mostly white people coded as tourists traveling through touristy markets, and many of us, indeed, are buying carpets. It makes sense for the carpet-sellers to assume we might be receptive to their products and come toward us. One day, three white men in our group, though, become personally offended by this assumption and get insulted. They start yelling at the vendors to "Leave us the hell alone!" and "We don't want your stuff!" They then proceed to shoo away all subsequent inter-actions with Moroccan vendors in public spaces with big, sweeping arm gestures and big shouts of "No! No! We don't want any!" People around us gape in surprise. The vendors slink away, chastised, humil-iated, and grumbling under their breath.

Another moment that stays with me takes place during our visit to the Hassan II Mosque in Casablanca. Our guide instructs the women in our group to cover our heads by wearing scarves to show respect to the worshippers in the mosque and broader compound area. A few of our participants resist this request to conform to local gen-dered norms. One person mutters comments about "those backward people" and how she as an American woman should not be subject to the same norms as Moroccan women. "I'm not one of them," she keeps insisting, the word "them" hard and pointed. "Why do I have to dress like them?" She eventually does drape the scarf over her head after alighting the bus, but only barely, and after a great deal of public affect. Our Moroccan guide becomes embarrassed at her behavior and remains withdrawn after the encounter. Another woman in our group continues to wear shorts on our excursions, even though she is told numerous times that women in Morocco do not wear shorts in public and it isn't culturally appropriate. "But I'm hot," is her reply.

As we travel around, I watch the ways local Moroccans watch us, and feel ashamed that the behavior of a few can define us as a whole.

Most of us are not insensitive and entitled Americans, but that is the general impression we are giving. A few of my friends on the program and I talk about our observations and discomforting feelings. Are we being hypercritical and oversensitive? Or are these actually rude instances born out of American entitlement that need to be checked? Whose responsibility in a group like ours, then, is it to check this?

We also talk about why some of us might act in ways we might normally not when we are abroad. Maybe our white male colleagues who really don't want carpets act up because they aren't used to being visibly flagged as "rich American tourists" and "the ones who represent wealth." Maybe they are more used to being unmarked and unremarkable, "ordinary and normal." Maybe a few of our white women colleagues, too, aren't sure how to conduct themselves as "liberated American women" in a country whose gender norms are visually different to what they are used to at home. Though we have classroom conversations on Islamic feminism and Moroccan women's rights, we need to talk about the visual codes some of us mistakenly assume are binary and universal (such as covering head = less freedom), and how our own cultural perspectives (and perhaps hubris) might be limiting our understanding. Nobody in our group is Muslim and many in our cohort have spoken openly of our unfamiliarity with Islam and Muslims in general. I wonder if and how our unconscious Western Islamophobia might also be affecting our interactions with local people as foreigners.

As a group, we never surface and speak about these cultural and identity issues, even though they are playing out for us constantly. A few of my colleagues and I ask the program director if we can convene a formal "unpacking identity" session to give us some time and space to talk about these issues together. We want a space to say what we are noticing and experiencing about being foreigners abroad in a heterogeneous and complex country. "If we have time, sure," was the noncommittal answer we receive, but that time never comes nor was made. On my own, I don't know how to begin a seemingly casual conversation over lunch about serious topics with the whole group, especially when some of the bad vibes I am feeling from our group seem to hinge on what local people say to me. I recognize a mere three-hour session couldn't reconcile all our feelings, but it would surely create a container for us to say aloud some of what is on our minds about traveling in a country and culture that is unfamiliar to most of us.

Without conversation on any of these identity, context, and cultural issues, it's no wonder a few of us become a bit less anchored and unhinged. Discomfort, without a productive valve to release it or a venue to talk it out, often manifests in less-than-productive ways. As a group, we stay silent and isolated, siloed in our feelings. And because we have no conversation on these underlying issues or behaviors, because they aren't spoken about or addressed, folks start to retreat within themselves and get increasingly touchy with each other, including me.

Local vendors continue to approach me and Ahmed throughout this time, but as I witness more moments in my group that make me cringe, I find myself changing my response. In a weird gesture to protect my fellow group members' sensitivities about race, culture, and identity, I begin to shrink away from the interactions with local Moroccans that I once relished. If someone approaches me as part of the "Sri Lanka? Somalia?" routine, I adopt an uncomprehending and vacant look, and skim my gaze over them with dull tolerance. The people who enthusiastically approach me see in my demeanor my recalcitrance to engage, and soon retreat with a disappointed sigh or shrug of their shoulder. When I realize what I am doing, I become contrite, angry, and all tangled up. What the hell am I doing? What kind of racial and cultural logic compels me to mute my excitement at talking with local people to cater to and protect my colleagues' sense of unease? Why do I have to be responsible for other people's discomfort? That shouldn't be my job, right? Is how local people react to me something I actually need to mitigate, something I need to handle on behalf of my white American traveling companions, some who are not, I feel, critically interrogating their own assumptions and reactions? I feel judgmental and indignant, but am not sure how to navigate the group dynamics and my own jumbled feelings.

I can't help but wonder how our journey might have played out differently if we had been encouraged as a group to say a bit of what was happening out loud. We needed a formal space to gather, and time to unpack and think through the larger issues that we were navigating but didn't mention. If we had talked together more intentionally, I can't totally be sure, but I have a strong feeling we all might have felt a bit better and had less reason to act out our anxieties. It would have been initially uncomfortable—we are, for the most part, unpracticed with these kinds of conversations. On the other hand, we certainly were already steeped in discomfort, but just weren't saying anything productive about it. Our silences can sometimes speak louder than our awkward, unskilled conversations.

- -

Holding Space Together

- Have you seen people in your group acting in ways that made you uncomfortable during your travels abroad? What were people doing? Why do you think they were behaving the ways they were? How did you navigate this?
- When you have traveled to another social context either close to home or far away and had to navigate differences in identity and experience, have you found yourself behaving in less than flattering ways as a mechanism to cope with feelings of

discomfort? How did that play out? What does it feel like thinking about that instance now with some distance and time?

- The term "Ugly American" is used to describe a set of behaviors that entitled tourists from the United States do when traveling abroad. Is there a corresponding "Ugly Australian," "Ugly Israeli," or "Ugly Bulgarian"? Why or why not? What kinds of actions would qualify as this?

- Canadian travelers have been known to sew the Canadian flag on their backpacks to avoid being mistaken for Americans. This speaks to the real fear of being seen as all the things that the term "Ugly American" connotes. Might some Canadians (or Australians or Israelis) feel a sense of relief that they are not American, and thus, feel superior and exempt from having to consider their own behavior abroad? What are your thoughts on this?

- What is the power of empathy? How have you witnessed empathy playing out in your own life? What might be the limits of empathy as well? If teaching empathy is a tricky task, knowing we've learned it too can be difficult to ascertain. How might we know we are empathetic, or empathetic enough?

When we share aloud what usually is privatized, we interrupt architectures of silence and shame by saying, "Oh, yes. That happened to me too." Such recognition can be powerful, and can grow our empathy in a complex world. As Helena Maria Viramontes notes in the introduction to *All About Skin: Short Stories by Women of Color*, "Empathy is the glue that makes the words of a writer stick to the reader, and in this era of globalization, understanding and feeling the life of another through narratives is a nonviolent act of sheer humane importance."

Fluid Identities and Mindful Travel

Though we go abroad to see others and ourselves with new eyes, we're somehow newly surprised each time the people we meet on our travels see us differently than we might be used to. Once we leave our own home contexts—and for some of us, even when we *are* at home—the usual ways we've imagined ourselves might not be so clear. Who you are essentially when you go abroad doesn't change, but how you are perceived and what that means for you and others might change. This shift can be extremely humbling—to realize that how you are viewed is determined, in large part, by where you are, who is around you, and which mythical norms are prioritized, glorified, and enforced. We are never fixed and immutable beings, but rather culturally and socially constructed at different moments throughout our lives. Although there's something comforting about feeling like we are already and always "ourselves" regardless of the outside environment, it's more accurate to think about our identities as unfinished and fluid, fluctuating and dependent on the context.

This fluidity offers us a useful theoretical model to consider how we move through the world both at home and abroad. This model could've been helpful for my colleagues and me during our time in Morocco. If we had begun to think about the ways that we are always shifting our sense of ourselves based on what's around us and people's

perceptions of us, we might have been more prepared for the ways that travel often knocks us flat on our backside. If we had become more comfortable with the idea that in an unfamiliar context— especially in the unequal world that we're a part of—*of course* people will see and interpret us in ways that may be jarring, difficult, or wonderful, perhaps we could have held steadier in those moments. With practice and familiarity, we might feel less shocked, more forgiving, less knotted up, and more like, "Yup, this happens," when situations unfold.

During our time in Morocco, we neither practiced nor stretched, nor were we encouraged to hold space or think of our identities as fluid and contextual. And it showed in the not-so-nice ways some of our apparently unprocessed emotions became externalized in our anxieties. Sharing our stories together—particularly white travelers and travelers of color sharing stories together—is very powerful: not just the gallant and funny stories we all might enjoy, but the discomforting, painful, and confusing ones that make us avert our eyes and not know what to say. Oftentimes, these are the stories that touch on issues of inequality and history, hierarchy and bias. In an unequal world, developing the skills to notice the ways these issues play out, and why our experiences as Western travelers are really dependent on what we look like, where in the world we are, what kinds of expectations people place on us, where those expectations come from, and how we respond and why all are parts of the process of traveling mindfully. Mindful travel is slowing down our thoughts and learning to stay with our feelings. Mindful travel is also sharing these uncomfortable stories in uncomfortable situations, and sitting with our discomfort.

I know it would have been powerful for me to hear directly from my white colleagues in Morocco. My empathy might have been better activated (and my snarky judgement reduced) if I had heard them say they were struggling in new and unfamiliar ways, and if they had space, courage, and humility to acknowledge some of the conflicting feelings they were experiencing as white men of a certain class with global advantage, or white feminists who had a particular notion of what "women's rights" meant and looked like to them. I also like to think it could have been equally important for these colleagues to better understand how Ahmed and I felt to be traveling in this larger group, also as Americans but very differently positioned because of our race, ethnicity, and global experiences. I know for me personally, the more judgmental or anxious I feel, the less open I am to nuance. Being a mindful traveler is all about appreciating the nuance, but it's hard to access if it's buried in angry chatter or disquieting inner noise. Imagine how our interactions with each other and local people might have been more intentional and centered if we'd had the chance to, at the very least, acknowledge and discuss the following:

- What it meant for some of us to be so visible when we're used to being "regular and ordinary"
- What gender norms here made us feel about gender norms back home
- What local people in different parts of the world assume "American" means
- How our expectations, stereotypes, and images about Muslims reconciled with the regular and ordinary Muslims we were interacting with daily
- How Ahmed and I felt to be seen in particular ways
- How our white colleagues felt to be seen from different angles
- Where all these assumptions in the first place come from

Though none of us on that trip could have changed the outer conditions of how people approached us, how they reacted to us, or what they said or did not, with some strategic conversation we could have turned toward ourselves and each other with more patience, understanding, and comradery.

- -

Holding Space Together

- What experiences in your life can you now see relating to the idea that identity is a process, always unfinished? How have you noticed that who you are in one context differs, morphs, or means different things elsewhere? Why might this be so?
- In her essay "How to Tame A Wild Tongue," Chicana poet, activist, and essayist Gloria Anzaldúa describes how the languages she speaks, her accent, expressions, and Mexican and American bi-culturality are routinely shamed and beaten out of her. People tried to tame her tongue, and she struggled to retain a sense of self. In dialogue with Ms. Anzaldúa, trans-lingual scholar Tamera Marko says, "I would say that it is not our tongues that need to be tamed: rather, it is our ears that need to be tuned."

  Consider what it might mean to "tame" the "wildness" out of each other's identities and experiences. What would it mean to "tune our ears" instead? How might this relate to the "Where are you from?" question discussed in the context of the friendly vendors, and the feelings it might invoke, however unintended and unconscious?
- If you were abroad and noticed that your group really needed a structured conversation on identity, difference, and power, how would you convince your program director or group leader to make the formal time and space for this important conversation?
- In his seminal book *Orientalism,* Edward Said writes, "The more one is able to leave one's cultural home, the more easily is one able to judge it, and the whole world as well, with the

spiritual detachment and generosity necessary for true vision. The more easily, too, does one assess oneself and alien cultures with the same combination of intimacy and distance." Reflect on what Said suggests with the evocative pairs "spiritual detachment and generosity," and "intimacy and distance." How do these phrases resonate for you?

CHAPTER 4

Ticket Bought, Part Two:
Friendship across Difference

Patted and Stroked: Attention Gained, Attention Lost

DOWN THE LIVELY STREETS OF RIO DE JANEIRO, BRAZIL, MY FRIEND and I linked arms. Everyday we'd start out early after a light breakfast of pao de queijo, hollow balls of bread touched with the tangy hint of cheese. We walked everywhere. The Biblioteca Nacional offered us the irrepressible scent of antiquity, while the beaches of Copacabana presented more surgically perfected breasts, bums, and buffness than I had ever seen. My favorite outings were when we strolled the outdoor plazas and markets. I noticed the combined vibrancy and desperation of trade taking place everywhere. It seemed that wherever we roamed, the majestic Sugarloaf Mountain rose to accompany us, a foggy yet friendly third companion to our winning twosome.

My friend and I were graduate students together in California. As this was her third archival research trip to Brazil, she was quite familiar with the city. I had come to Rio purely on holiday to visit her and sightsee. White with light skin, my friend had learned Portuguese and spoke the language well. I, on the other hand, knew very little about Brazil and spoke no Portuguese. We had met years before on campus and shared a dislike for the interminable meetings we were forced to sit through as teaching assistants. In our scholarly work, we both focused on issues of race, history, and representation, and quickly grew close. The sweet notes of affection we left for each other in the department mailroom cemented our friendship.

One day, parched from our city walk through Rio, we rested at a small café. My friend approached the lady behind the counter and began to order in Portuguese.

"*Bom Día, Senhora.* Good day to you. One café com leite and one cup of tea with milk, please. Brigada." I joined my friend at the counter. We stood together smiling politely, waiting for our refreshments. We needed caffeine. Desperately.

"I can give you café com leite but no tea with milk," the Senhora says.

The Senhora first glanced at my friend. She slowly switched her gaze to me. And then she studied both of us, in one frame, as a pair. I noticed she hadn't begun to prepare our drinks. The Senhora lowered her face closer to me like a construction crane, and in a rapid stream of enthusiasm, began to speak. "[Lots of Portuguese that I did not understand.]"

Apologetically, I replied with the one Portuguese sentence I had practiced: "*Desculpe, eu não falo português.* Sorry, I do not speak Portuguese. But she does," I say, pointing helpfully back to my friend.

By now, the Senhora had all but vaulted over the counter to get closer to me. In the process she repositioned my friend a few feet over, and grabbed my arm. "*Você é tão bonita!*" the Senhora exclaimed.

My friend giggled and then translated, "Oh, your skin is so beautiful! You are the perfect mix of black and white!"

The Senhora then began to stroke the skin on my face and arms. Up and down my body she stroked. "Oh, this brown. Look at this color brown!" she gushed, up and down, up and down.

"Holy crap," I thought. "What is this lady doing?" Wooden with awkwardness, I felt my polite smile melt down my face. Did skin stroking—especially the skin of strangers—constitute a cultural thing here, I wondered? Was she really touching me so boldly? And where were our drinks?

"*Com licença, Senhora.* Actually, she's not Brazilian. She's from India," my friend interjected. The sentence seemed to slip by the Senhora, still mesmerized as she was by the apparent magic of my skin. My friend valiantly pressed on. "She's not Brazilian. She's from India. You know India? It's far away. Near China. That's why she's brown." I loved my friend for explaining my brownness to our café lady, a brownness that rooted me in a context outside the one unfolding in front of us.

The Senhora now nodded in the direction of where my friend stood, yet continued to cling to my arms. The lady sure had a strong grip. Up and down, she stroked my skin for another few moments, and more Portuguese paragraphs poured from her. My friend and I caught glances and laughed at the oddness of the moment. Many, many more minutes passed before we received our beverages.

Throughout my visit to Rio de Janeiro, some version of this particular scenario occurred over and over again. I received an inordinate amount of what seemed to me to be unwarranted attention. Local Cariocas on the bus, on the road, in the shops exclaimed, "Oh, your color brown!" and my skin was commented on, handled, patted, and stroked. It's not like all Cariocas gave the brownness or me their attention. But the Cariocas who did focus on the brownness *Really Focused On The Brownness.* During the first few times this happened, I had stiffened into a stoic cement pole, unsure if I should snatch back my personal space and peel my arm away.

After some time, though, I relaxed more playfully as I learned to predict the familiar interactions. I realized that the Cariocas who ran their hands up and down my body did so with little intention to be rude, inappropriate, or seductive. They just really seemed to dig the brownness, for something about it was neither solely black nor white, but an unmistakable mixture of the two. Skin-strokers repeatedly exhorted, "This color is the best kind of Brazilian," visually highlighting the racial history of Brazil peopled with African slaves and Portuguese slave holders. I began to wonder if the skin-strokers unconsciously imagined my brownness as a hopeful proof of multicultural triumph, even though Brazil remained steeped in visible and persistent economic and racial inequality. For days, my friend served as translator during these skin-stroking encounters. I lost count of how many times I felt unfamiliar hands run up and down my body, and how many times I heard my friend say, "India. You know India? Near China."

While I remained preoccupied reflecting on the social phenomena of my skin color, another dynamic was playing out in every skin-stroking encounter:

1) Though I spoke no Portuguese, many of the interactions my friend and I had with local people centered around me and my brownness.

2) My dear friend ended up oddly ignored or sidelined, often literally pushed away from the frame of focus even though it was her translations and cross-cultural skills that made the interactions possible. This brown-loving, skin-stroking, ignoring-my-friend thing happened almost every time we ventured out, and quickly became *A Thing*.

When Awkwardness and Discomfort Strike, Dig into the Research

To help make sense of the interactions—and to deflect the feelings we were starting to experience about being oddly celebrated or ignored—my friend and I dove into the heady and disembodied realm of academia. Years in graduate school had drilled into us the importance of critical distance from one's subject of study. And so we capped a lid on the weird feelings we were feeling and instead, busied ourselves with talk about contemporary Brazilian racial and social relations.

At first, talk about race and society in Brazil consumed us, for there's a lot to discover and discuss. Brazil is one of the most ethnically diverse countries in the world with populations descended from Indigenous Peoples, Europeans, and Africans; any casual visitor can see that Brazilians are all shades and combinations of white, brown, and black. An estimated four million enslaved Africans were brought to Brazil from Angola and other parts of Western Africa. This was, I learned, ten times the number of people brought to the United States under slavery. Currently, ninety-seven million African descendants call Brazil home, the largest number of Black people outside of Africa. I had always heard that Brazil operated as a racial democracy by encouraging racial mixing, and was thus better able to deal with its violent and oppressive origins than the United States. Was this true?

While racial mixing in Brazil did not always have the social stigma that has defined the US racial landscape, all was definitely not well. Contemporary Brazilian Blacks often do not have access to the education, healthcare, and economic resources that lighter-skinned Brazilians enjoy. My friend explained this critique of the racial harmony myth, and shared with me articles and books that described how light-skinned Brazilians continue to be privileged and hold a disproportionate share of wealth and power throughout the country.

In addition to the history and sociology we read and discussed, my friend and I also investigated racial imagery in art and culture. Once, we spent the day at a conference center poring over a multimedia exhibit commemorating four hundred years of African presence in the country. Multiple tents and vast halls brought together thousands of artifacts, testimonies, documents, quilts, and paintings. One image in particular greeted us at the entrance of the largest hall. Modesto Brocos' iconic 1895 painting *The Redemption of Ham*, features three generations of a multiracial Brazilian family: a Black grandmother, her mixed-race mulatta daughter, the daughter's white spouse, and their light-skinned white baby. The mother and father gaze at their baby, while the dark-skinned grandmother stands to the left with her hands raised in prayer, thanking God that her grandson is white. Brocos' painting provided a graphic representation of the racial whitening concepts that my friend and I had been discussing.

And Then, the Dumb Fight on the Subway Platform

Our copious research offered my friend and me the semblance of control, but our academic theories and five-syllable words served only to cover our feelings. At first it had worked; our loquacious talk had swept away the awkwardness we had started to feel during the skin-stroking episodes. But corked feelings of discomfort about race, identity, and difference tend to explode and spill over if unattended. How to uncork the container of weird, messy feelings we didn't know how to discuss? We knew neither how to sit in the discomfort of our own truths or what it would mean to listen and see things from each other's perspective. Our fear of a potentially uncomfortable conversation stifled us, and we marinated in silent irritation.

Until one night, when all our feelings didn't delicately bubble forth but gushed us sopping wet. It started quite innocuously. We stood on a subway station platform on the northern side of Rio.

"Are we going to take this train home, or the next one?" I had asked. My voice must have rung rusty with irritation. Our fight had started out small, in fact. Petty, even. A simple miscommunication about plans for the evening.

"I thought we were going to the concert," my friend had replied, slightly peeved at my apparent disregard for the thoughtful plans she had made for us. "Isn't that what we had decided earlier today?"

"We've done everything you have wanted," I snapped back, quickly and irrationally esca- lating us into soggy territory. "It doesn't matter what I say," I pouted. "In fact, I can't say much here as I don't speak the language, in case you forgot." I felt wronged and sorry for myself.

My friend took in my sour expression and returned the scowl. "What are you talking about? I've translated for you every second of every day you've been here!" she exclaimed. And even though technically she was right, I didn't care.

We continued to stand on the platform and eye each other. I might have yelled some more. And finally, thankfully, horribly, the things we had assiduously avoided talking about the last few days whooshed out of us.

"I've been doing everything for you here! Why aren't you a bit more grateful?"

"Grateful? I thought you'd be learning something about race with all these interactions we've been having. Seems like you're not the grateful one!"

"You're the one whose ego has irrepressibly swelled just because people here seem to like your color. This isn't about you!"

"Of course it is! This is about me, and it's about you. This is

about what it means to be white, and the difficulty you're having to share the spotlight with a woman of color!" I started to walk away.

"I haven't shared the spotlight with you in any way!" she retorted, voice hard. "I've been pushed out of it altogether, in case you haven't noticed!"

Once the dam burst, we lurched toward all the hurt and confusion we had been feeling. But as in the way of burst dams, our talk was neither careful nor strategic, just explosive. We felt relief at speaking what needed to be spoken, but I'm sure we—and especially I—could have been gentler and kinder. Speaking what-needs-to-be-spoken does not immunize any of us from the consequences of speaking what-needs-to-be-spoken-but-rarely-gets-voiced.

On that obstreperous night on the subway platform, the walk home later, and for many days afterward, we both wondered privately: could our friendship withstand such battering? I asked myself: how could I take back the foul things I uttered while also insisting that something significant about race and whiteness and racial identity had brought us to this point? Were all conversations about race, power, and identity destined to end in irrational, dumb exchanges on a subway platform and a bruised friendship? Both my friend and I tackled issues of race in our work and thought of ourselves as progressive anti-racists. How could things have gone so badly between us? And because we weren't sure how to say any of this out loud, we continued to visit museums and exhibitions, book stores and beaches, now more quiet in our speech, more careful in our demeanor. In the distance, the image of Sugarloaf Mountain followed us in companionate silence, ever present, a touchstone from which to return.

Whiteness and Brownness in a Complicated Racial Mix

Somewhere along the way, the experience of being ignored and perceived as an accessory to my "perfect brownness" wore my friend down. I can see that now. This erasure must have been painful for her. I know of the careful and conscientious way in which she first entered Brazilian culture as a US white woman and cultural outsider. I imagine the frustration she must have felt when her knowledge and sensitivity were repeatedly sidelined. She was the one who had years of experience with Brazil, not me. She breathed in Brazilian history and navigated the contemporary streets, not me. She spoke Portuguese, not me. And yet within our social interactions, she was rendered secondary during our skin-stroking encounters.

But—and here's the complicated part—in a wider Brazilian framework, that same whiteness and North Americanness undoubtedly opened doors and opportunities for her. As a white woman from the United States in a society that continues to associate European roots with social and economic privilege as well as the symbolic status of whiteness, my friend fit the bill and benefited from her racial background and looks. But strangely, during the skin-stroking incidents we experienced, the whiteness that in other ways benefited her seemed to take a backseat to something else. It didn't make much sense to us. How could the explicitly celebrated whiteness—think back to that famous Brazilian painting of the dark-skinned grandmother praising the Lord for lightening her grandbaby—also be something to ignore in favor of a brownness that, ostensibly, seemed different and less valuable than white?

I, on the other hand, at first delighted that the brownness that had marked me as Other in the United States had suddenly transformed into a *Quality To Be Fawned Over* asset. Never did I think that my particular skin color could elicit such explicitly positive reactions from so many people. I was used to my skin color receiving curious reactions from local people, as when I traveled through Morocco or China. I was also familiar with neutral or no reactions to my color, or in some cases, negative reactions for being too dark or straight up racism and discrimination for not being white. Now, in Brazil, had I slipped into a magical world where my skin color garnered straight up appreciation? The attention got to my head. While I did notice that the skin-stroking Cariocas tended to bypass my friend as they made a beeline for me, I hadn't put too much energy into analyzing how she might feel. I thought only of myself, and rationalized my bad behavior by telling myself that the continued benefits of her whiteness both in the United States and even in Brazil should keep her grateful and happy. And if she did feel a bit miffed, I reasoned, shouldn't this experience of being temporarily overlooked deepen her understanding of what institutional white privilege felt like to many people of color in a US context? Couldn't she see that now, finally, the compliments and attention I received were a small reversal of fortune?

Overlapping Truths, or How Hurt People Can Also Hurt People

I cringe now when I think of how I acted back then. I wasn't totally wrong, but I also wasn't totally right either. Both my friend and I were valid in our complex emotions, although we did not have the skills to embrace the messiness of the larger historical and racial dynamic in which we found ourselves.

When Audre Lorde described her concept of the mythical norm, she also said this: "Those of us who stand outside that power often identify one way in which we are different, and we assume that to be the primary cause of all oppression, forgetting other distortions around difference, some of which we ourselves may be practicing." Lorde's quote reveals many overlapping truths—that while our own differences and distance from the mythical norm might cause us hurt, we ourselves might hurt others based on their differences that might look different than what we are used to recognizing. Figuring out how to balance our own privileges and oppressions can be a lifelong process.

From the close friendship my friend and I have continued to share since our time together in Brazil along with my extended travels and readings about race, I know now that whiteness as a racial identity is always complicated by class and gender and many other identities. Isolating race—and insisting that someone is privileged or not solely by a racial structure—obfuscates the more nuanced way that all our identities intersect and make us intersectional. In my friend's case, her experience of an advantaged identity in one category of her life (race) has always been mediated by the ways she has had to negotiate the less-advantaged aspects of her life (gender and class).

For me, the racism I had experienced in the United States or the negative "Isn't it a shame that you're so dark" comments I had received were also mediated by the many real advantages in my own life, privileges of class and education and citizenship status. I can never admit to being only oppressed or marginalized, because that's just not true. I have had and continue to enjoy incredible advantages. Just like my friend, my many identities and experiences both visible and less visible manifest throughout my life. Realizing the interconnectedness of both my friend and me has helped me expand my ideas of how power and privilege work in sometimes obvious and sometimes less-obvious ways. Cultural theorist Kobena Mercer reminds us that our task is "to theorize more than one difference at a time," for there are always different kinds of difference and advantage playing out all at once.

The fight on the subway platform helped me learn that just because my friend was white in an institutional system that afforded her historic and contemporary advantages over other skin colors did not mean that she was immune to feeling hurt and snubbed by the very racial system which conferred benefits on her. Racism hurts us all. It strips each of us of the enjoyment of our full potential, and it prevents us from enjoying the full potential of each other. Our experiences with racism, though, are not the same based on who we are and how we intersect with history—racism hurts us all differently.

I also realized that just because I had sometimes felt othered and differentiated on account of my own skin color did not mean I got a free pass to act badly with my white friend. History matters—absolutely—as do institutional structures that uphold discrimination and bias, but so does being humane and kind to the people around us. Both my friend and I, yes, were differently placed within US and Brazilian racial systems because of our different identities. But we were also just regular people with tender feelings that needed to be appreciated and safeguarded. Both of us needed to treat the other with care and compassion, especially because of the ways that race is complicated and at times, contradictory. Our fear of initiating necessary and honest conversation petrified us. Our discomfort led to less open talking, and less open talking led to more judgement.

Friendship Regained: Listening and Learning

The memory of feeling uncomfortable and knotted up has stayed with me for many years. I feel both disappointed in myself at how my discomfort and anxiety manifested in a less-than-generous stance with my friend, and also incredibly proud that she and I worked through our hurt feelings together. It took some time, and it certainly wasn't easy. We waded through the awkwardness, neither of us sure where our friendship would end up.

Cross-racial friendships are bound to evidence the scars of a pro-foundly unequal history and present. How could our friendship—or any cross-racial relationship for that matter—*not* experience hiccups along the way, given the confusing, painful, oppressive, and long-lasting institutional and personal ramifications of race and racism around the world? We did recognize this history during our many post-subway-platform conversations. Both of us were racialized in an unequal racial environment, the same way all of us are gendered within an unequal gendered environment. These structures of race and gender, and other kinds of differences, don't just affect how we relate to one another on a personal level, but manifest in the structures and institutions that govern our lives, including education, medical care, housing, employment, and beauty standards. They structure how we see ourselves and each other both consciously and uncon-sciously. When my friend and I took a few breaths and understood *of course* structural issues permeate personal relationships, we were able to approach the situation and each other with more generosity. The knowledge that broad-scale structural issues about race, beauty, and hierarchy affect personal relationships somehow gave us permission to de-escalate our disagreement. Our fight didn't just happen because we (or I, really) behaved badly. Yes, I could've responded better to the discomfort I felt, but I was also responding to the discomfort that is already so palpable in society. How could I, my friend, or any-one, really, know how to effectively or perfectly work out in our own minds and personal relationships what we haven't as a society been able to solve for hundreds of years?

Reflecting on this incident years later, I'm also struck by the gaps between what we know and knowing better, how much we think we know and what is really unknowable. As someone who has been thinking about issues of identity and difference for a long time, I sometimes feel I should know what to do in awkward moments when I experience different kinds of difference. This is absolutely not the case. Sometimes, the differences I've found abroad or at home feel sweet and light and friendly. Other times, the differences I experience feel heavy and restrictive, like a thick chain winding around my limbs. I haven't always known what to do or say in uncomfortable moments, or how to acknowledge the escalating conflict and discomfort I can feel within me. That's still the case now. Over time, though, I've developed more grace, allowing me to feel better about being wrong and admitting that sometimes I actually know very little.

In Brazil, these nascent critical realizations helped me ramp down my ego and highlight the care and connection I wanted to nurture with my friend. I slowed down my mental judgement and interrupted the narratives of hurt I had repeated to myself like a warm refrain. I was surprised to notice that as I became more comfortable acknowledging my deeper wounds, my own wrongdoing, and how I wanted to grow, my friend and I had more space in our friendship for deep listening. She, too, stepped toward me with openness and vulnerability. We both grew, and felt the deep satisfaction of being heard.

None of us have a manual for dealing with the different ways our differences and advantages make us feel, or how our identities might play out abroad or at home. We do, however, have small choices of how we navigate what and who might be in front of us. In the process of attending more carefully with each other and listening to each other's stories, we might even heal a bit of ourselves.

CHAPTER 5

- - - - - - - - - - - - - - - -

I Thought I Was Here to Look at You:
Story Clusters

I OFTEN THINK OF THE TIME I SPENT IN MOROCCO, AND IMAGINE THE kind of cross-racial story-sharing and holding space that could've been helpful for me and my colleagues. Perhaps you have similar imaginings of journeys you've previously taken. So, how do we get to the place where we can make these imaginings reality?

We can practice listening and holding stories, especially across race and experience. There's no single story when it comes to the Western travel experience, whether you identify as a person of color, white, mixed race, or none of the above. The ways we make sense of our identities often shift when we are abroad and oblige us to see ourselves and others differently. Each of our stories are personally ours and unique, for sure, but they also reflect the broader systems of structural advantages, unconscious biases, and local and global hierarchies that you and I participate in and travel through.

This chapter provides a crash course in such traveling stories that touch on inequality and history, racial hierarchy and bias. The following short stories—some only a paragraph in length—portray fifteen travelers' reflections on what it means to be seen, fit in, and acknowledged for who we are (or not). We'll focus on how the situation makes the traveler feel, and widen our gaze to consider what social and historical factors caused the situation to occur in the first place. Though the fifteen short stories overlap thematically, I've grouped them into four clusters so we can concentrate on a particular subject or issue.

I offer these stories as a medley of voices, perspectives, and emotions. Like a juggler who's gradually learning to incorporate more and more balls into her act, holding many stories in our minds and hearts at once requires us to stretch, absorb, and grow. When we take in and reflect on travel experiences that might be different from ours, it helps us to travel more mindfully, recognizing that our story might not be the only story worth knowing.

Cluster 1: "People Thought They Knew Me": Stereotyping

Though race is only one feature of our identity, it's often how we're first recognized by others and thus is one of the quickest ways we consciously and unconsciously categorize each other. That's why I've focused on race in this book. Western travelers might feel knotted up with confusion and frustration on account of how our race is perceived. At the same time, this very identity that confounds us in one moment might make you and me feel strangely and sheepishly special in other ways as well. As with most, if not all of these clusters, the first three stories are personal and unique, and yet more universal than the person they feature.

> ERIC: "People on the street who see me certainly don't know me as Eric Johnson. They don't know anything

about me except my skin color, which makes me very recognizable," says Eric, an African American man, about his time in Guangdong, China. I am in Beijing for a few days and meet him at a temple. He's on break from his work in Guangdong, and is touring Beijing, like me, as a sightseer. "It's almost like I'm too recognizable, sometimes. People think they know me, or they want to know me, only because I'm Black." He looks away and says, "If people do actually talk to me, I'm never really sure why they're approaching me. Sometimes it might be only because I'm Black and they have a particular image of what I'll be like from the movies and sports. Everyone here thinks I play basketball and that I'm not that smart. Sometimes people ask me when I came from Africa. One person even asked me if I have AIDS because I'm Black! People think they know who I am and what I am, but the thing is, most Chinese don't know much about me or other Black people at all besides two or three stereotypes. I know I can't get too caught up in how people see me, but it gets tiring always trying to figure this stuff out."

JOHN: John is a white American friend who has worked in South Asia in the development sector. "Nobody knew me," John says of his time traveling in Pakistan. "No one knew me as an actual person, but people thought they knew me because of how I look. I am just me, but I'm starting to realize that in Pakistan I represented white people in Hollywood and American TV shows. I represented wealthy people, a wealthy nation, and a powerful military presence in the region. Nobody knew me personally, but my white skin made people assume they knew me and what I was about."

ELSA: Elsa, a Swedish graduate student, is doing fieldwork in rural Indonesia for her dissertation. She shares her story in a global health workshop that I am attending. "I've noticed how my appearance seems to offer me speedier service at shops and on the road," she says. "Last month in the field, the storekeeper rang my purchases up first even though there were several local people standing around who were there before I came along. I was the only foreigner and white person around, and it was clear to everyone that my speedier service was because of this fact alone. Nobody seemed angry, but I sure felt uncomfortable. What am I supposed to do in that moment? Say, 'Thanks, but no thanks?' or just smile politely and slink away after I've been invited to blatantly cut the line on account of my foreigner status and skin color?" Elsa feels her exasperation and shame mix together. "It's hard to admit that even though moments like this make me uncomfortable, and I feel bad saying this, there's a part of me that also enjoyed the special treatment."

Both at home and abroad, sometimes our visible identities are categorized as "less than," and we are viewed and treated poorly. Sometimes, our visible identities are categorized as "something better or special," and we are viewed and treated better than others around us. A student of mine named Emily once said that sometimes we are perceived as a "hero" with positive attention, and sometimes, more of a "zero" with negative or less attention. Sometimes, we may not be viewed or treated explicitly poorly or better than others, but somehow, just *differently* than the other people around us. And at still other times, parts of our visible identities just might not be that big of a deal to the people we meet. Any of these experiences can make us feel irritable, on display, relieved, hurt, special, out of sorts, or somewhat confused—whoever you are—because it's disorienting to realize how much of our identity is externally determined, especially coming from a culture that emphasizes how much identity is our own, something to be chosen.

Holding Space Together

• Based on who we are and how we are perceived, we must differently navigate our similarities, differences, and the broader power structures like racism, patriarchy, and homophobia. But take a moment to reflect on why and how both white travelers and travelers of color may experience similar feelings of surprise, guilty delight, or having-to-represent-our-entire-group during parts of their trips abroad.

I don't mean to flatten all our experiences and say that all white travelers and travelers of color will have similar experiences abroad, or even that all white travelers or all travelers of color will experience travel the same way. What I do mean, rather, is that even with our important differences in identity, experience, and how we are perceived and treated, Western travelers of many races may feel similarly to one another from time to time—this based on the history that affects our present and the mythical norms of the society we are encountering. How may this reflection help us make better sense of our experiences and of the actions and reactions of those traveling with us?

- In both Eric's and John's stories, the travelers are male and therefore they are dealing with the mythical norm in terms of gender. Their gender is considered "ordinary and regular," something they might not have had to pay much attention to. How might each of their stories be similar or different if one or both of the travelers were a Black or white woman?

- You'll notice that although Eric, John, and Elsa are all hyper-visible and approached by local people because of their racial appearance, the images and stereotypes that are associated with their race differ dramatically in each of the scenarios. Being seen as "powerful and wealthy" or "more special than locals and thus subject to special treatment," is quite different than being seen as "only good at sports" or "having a stigmatized condition."

  How might John and Elsa—white people on the receiving end of conscious and unconscious advantages based on their skin colors—stretch themselves to listen carefully and hold Eric's story without deflecting their discomfort? What would it mean for them to say aloud some of the conflicting feelings they are experiencing? What might encourage Eric to share parts of his story with Elsa and John, people both like him and unlike him in different ways?

- One of the trickiest skills to develop when we're interacting with others abroad is the capacity to know if something is happening because we're an outsider and a representative of the West, or if this same interaction would have happened regardless of any identifiable feature of our foreignness and appearance. What are ways we might develop and deepen this skill?

Cluster 2: Being Seen and Un-Seen: The Power of Whiteness Abroad

As the first cluster of stories suggests, the color of our skin—and the various meanings associated with it—affect our traveling gait more than we realize or openly discuss. For many Western white or light-skinned travelers, the experience of being so explicitly noticed on account of skin color during global jaunts can come as a shock, given the implicit normalization of whiteness in the West. Something about whiteness and its link to wealth and power in majority Black and brown less-resourced lands can seem more visceral and tangible for many whites unused to explicitly being seen by their race at home.

These next six short stories continue to explore the different ways that the racial assumptions we're subjected to (as well as assumptions about gender, geographical origins, class status, among others) affect our travels abroad. How would you respond if you were hearing these stories from a classmate or a colleague or a close friend? How might we empathize with the storyteller and also pan out to better understand the broader social dynamics that give rise to these uncomfortable moments? Can we practice sharing and holding space through reading these stories?

> JANE: "Me being white here in India, well, it feels really different than me being white in Canada," says a white woman undergraduate named Jane I meet in India. She's studying abroad in the western part of the country. "In my home town, almost everybody is white. I never thought much about who I was. Here in India, though, it's kind of a big deal. People come up to me, want to talk with me and take a photo with me. People will just plop their babies into my arms and want a photo with me carrying their kid! It was pretty weird and unnerving at first, but I've got to

admit I also kind of love the attention I'm receiving." Jane rests for a moment and reflects. "I'm just a regular person at home, but here, I'm a celebrity without doing anything at all. It's strange, but wow—what an incredible experience to have people approach me solely because of the way I look!" Her voice is exuberant and breathy. "That's never happened to me before at home. I've always had to do something to be recognized back home. Here, just being me is enough to feel special."

PETER: "During my Peace Corps stay in Sierra Leone, I worked on a rural education project," says Peter, a friend of mine who's a white man from the United States in his mid-forties. "That was over twenty years ago, and I often was the only white person in the area. I quickly realized that everything I did was public knowledge: who I talked to, what I ate for breakfast, if I had a good shit or not, who I met at the market—all of it. Everything I did and everywhere I went was public knowledge. I've never been in a situation like this, where my actions and whereabouts were not only interesting to others but discussion worthy. I felt like a movie star with the paparazzi all around me. What a rough transition when I returned back to the US and realized nobody gave a shit about my shits!" He laughs, and continues. "I've reflected a lot on those experiences, and think it's made me a more careful thinker. I've continued to have a wide network of friends across race, and think that those early experiences in West Africa when I was younger helped me be more humble and less serious. I still make mistakes and mess up, of course, but I'm also not taken by surprise when uncomfortable things come up."

SAMMY: Sammy is a queer white woman traveler who had been sick with an intestinal virus while abroad in Bolivia. Her short hair is dyed a radiant purple, and her nose is pierced twice. She's a former student of mine, and shares what happened to her: "One afternoon at a rural clinic in Bolivia, a woman followed me into the bathroom to shake my hand and find out my name—even though I was holding a plastic container filled with a fresh stool sample. I know that I look different than most of the people here, but I am still not used to being stared at all the time. I sometimes do like the attention I receive, but I am realizing how comfortable I feel in Seattle being more anonymous, even with my hair the way it is."

Western travelers of color and especially dark-skinned people, in addition to navigating racial systems of power at home that structurally favor white and light-skinned people, might also experience similar things on their travels abroad via globally circulating race-based stereotypes and assumptions. Local people might treat us with suspicion, curiosity, friendliness, ambivalence, or even hostility. Though we might travel far, the racial hierarchies we sometimes find at home in the West are quite present elsewhere as well.

JASMINE: "I feel excluded in the US in more subtle, hard to prove ways," a Filipina American student named Jasmine writes in a journal assignment during one of my programs. "Here in India, it's more explicit. Some Indians flock toward the white people in our group and ask if they can take a photo, leaving me and the other folks of color by the wayside. I've literally been gently pushed out of the camera's frame because local people wanted to take a photo with my white classmates. It's not everyone here, mind you. Lots of Indians really don't care about foreigners or white people and just go about their business, so I get that it's not everyone. But being excluded from a photograph even a couple of times is still powerful. I knew race and racism as complex ideas in the US, but I didn't realize how these ideas also shaped cultures around the world until this trip.

"There are so many images of light-skinned Indians everywhere in India even though skin shades are from light to very dark. Where are all the dark-skinned people in media? The fairness creams I used to see in the Philippines when I was younger never used to freak me out until now. I guess I never thought about them too much. Pale-skinned Indians and Filipinos both dominate media and are visibly associated with wealth, beauty, or power, regardless if the norm in a particular region is dark skin. When will white fall out of fashion? I think I've learned more about whiteness and white culture while being in India and the Philippines, more than I could have ever imagined."

LAYLA: A mixed-race African and Asian American student named Layla is on a study abroad program in France and shares a homestay room with her white classmate. Layla told this story to her professor who's a friend of mine, who then shared the details with me as an example. The homestay family members are nice, but they seem more comfortable with the white student. When Layla and her white classmate return home from program activities, the family focuses on the white classmate. They ask her about her day, practice French with her, and offer to take her out on the weekend to local sights. To Layla, they are polite but guarded, polite without being warm. Layla talks to her professor about the situation and how she's feeling. "I'm not sure what to do. There's nothing specifically *wrong* since the family has provided all the things they're supposed to do as a homestay family. But yes, it's clear that they are much friendlier to my roommate and pretty neutral to me."

Layla pauses to collect her thoughts. "I get the feeling that they are more comfortable with my roommate and relate better to her because she's white and more like them. Maybe they just don't know what to do or say with me because I'm Black. I don't want to make my roommate feel bad, cuz it's not her fault the family is this way. But I just wish she'd notice and say something. I'm nervous to bring it up and draw more attention to this as I'm the only person of color on this program. I don't want to make a big deal about a 'feeling' I have that the homestay family likes the white girl more than me. And plus, if I'm right, what am I supposed to do about it?"

SUNNY: Sunny is a Black Canadian woman who I met at a writing workshop for people of color. She tells me about her time in Italy the year before. "No matter how I was dressed, how I was standing, what I was doing, or where I was going, when Italian men saw me on my own, many would think I was a sex worker," she says. "I was there for a month-long language immersion program, and got quite accustomed to the cat calls, the kissing noises, and the stares. The white girls on our program were often approached by Italian men too, but with me there seemed to be an edge to the attention I received. It made me feel so uncomfortable and unsafe. When I was on my own, I can't tell you how many times men asked me how much I charge. I am used to subtle Canadian racism. But this kind of in-your-face stuff, I never got used to this. It felt so patriarchal and almost violent. How am I supposed to read Italian literature and practice my language skills when all this other stuff keeps happening?"

Many of the stories in this cluster speak to the increased validation and desirability of light or white or fair skin abroad—even, paradoxically, when the racial and ethnic norms of a region are not that. I find it agonizingly sad that these histories continue both consciously and unconsciously in so many places. This is, of course, how the complicated history of whiteness and its associations play out in our contemporary world and cause so many of us pain. As Kamal Al-Solaylee writes in his book *Brown: What Being Brown in the World Today Means (to Everyone)*, "My struggles to feel at ease in the skin I'm in reflect global issues and trends that go beyond the personal. Everywhere I looked, every story I heard, all but confirmed the prejudices and advantages that a skin tone can inflict or bestow on individuals, communities, and nations." Many factors contribute to the valorization of whiteness abroad: colonial and imperial histories; the imposition and self-adoption of the colonizer's norms; contemporary global advertising that equates light and white and fair skin with wealth, prestige, and social mobility; and the global reach and fanfare of Hollywood, US music videos, global advertising, and other media representations.

And yet: You and I are just regular people in this broader system. We did not create any of the business-as-usual systems we find ourselves in abroad or at home. And yet: we bear the burdens of this system unequally depending on our identities and the persistent mythical norms around us. No wonder it sometimes feels as if we're at odds with one another when we try to talk about these issues. Or, when not at odds, we as a people are unsure how to wrap our minds around the complexities and complicities of how we should live together in an unequal world.

How, then, do we hold seemingly opposite stories together? The experiences of Jane, the white Canadian woman who is thrilled to receive requests to pose in photographs with local people's babies, are intimately yoked to the experiences of Jasmine, the Asian American woman who is pushed out of the photographic frame, also in India. How, too, might we come to understand that systems of power maintain the status quo in many ways, both subtle and blatant? Layla's sense that her French homestay family is more comfortable with her white roommate than with her could reflect the ways that our unconscious biases favor the people who are like us. As a child, my daughter might have experienced the sweet side of this phenomenon as she bonded with the African American couple at the choir show, but Layla's disconnect from the warm bonds forged between the homestay family and her white roommate illustrate another side to this. The sexualized racism that Sunny experiences in Italy is based on such assumptions, but feels more violent and visceral. Both situations leave Layla and Sunny alone to figure out what to do with their feelings and how to carry this forward. It's not any of our faults that these experiences take place, and yet, mindful travel in an unequal world reminds us that we are all differently placed within these systems.

- -

Holding Space Together

- As a white traveler, experiencing your race for the first time must indeed be striking, possibly shocking. Each of the three stories featuring this theme touch on the idea of privilege, sometimes directly and sometimes indirectly, both while abroad and while home. What are the differences in the travelers' reactions and reflections? How might being so visible in this way make a traveler feel especially guilty or guiltily special? (Do you think there is something significant about two of the stories of being white abroad discussing the intimate and usually private experience of using the toilet?)

- Sammy's bright purple hair is definitely eye catching, as are the two nose rings she's sporting. She's also a white woman in an area of the world where there are not that many white people.

  When Bolivians approach her, they might be curious about her hair, her jewelry, her gender expression, *or* her race: How is she (or we, for that matter) to know what is drawing people toward her? Are her experiences about race, gender, or are they about her unique purple hair and nose rings? Does it actually matter? Why or why not?

  We are the sum of our parts, for sure, but it's sometimes difficult to know in which order our parts are being summed.

- Talking about race and across racial differences can be slippery and tough. We each experience the world differently based on who we are. An unfair and entrenched system makes life so much harder for too many people, through racism or patriarchy, for example. And then there are the people who seem not to have to carry that burden, such as white people and men. And yet, none of us created this system. What are your thoughts on this?

  How can men and women come together to talk about patriarchy and gendered double standards? How might white people and people of color come together to talk about racist histories and how these influence our present? How might who you are—your identities and experiences in life—shape your views on these issues? How do we productively talk about systems of power with people who acquire benefits from the system alongside people who do not?

- There's a big difference between, say, men who ask lewdly, "How much for a night?" every time you are out in Italy, and a woman who places her child in your arms for a photo in India. And yet both situations exist because of the assumptions people make about who we are in the world and what our gendered whiteness or Blackness might mean to them.

  When is it okay to let something slide because as foreigners there is so much we don't know about what we are seeing? When, though, do you feel it would be worthwhile to say something and push back? Have you been in a situation where you wanted to say something but didn't? Or where you did say something?

  Noticing the dynamics of power, race, and identity helps us better understand the uncomfortable situations we might find ourselves in. Noticing these broader dynamics can also help us contextualize why the people we meet might act the way they do and can help us respond appropriately from our side.

- Sensitive Western travelers hope to be culturally appropriate and not come off as entitled. That doesn't mean, though, that we acquiesce to be in unsafe scenarios for fear we'll offend someone. Our safety and wellbeing are of utmost importance.

  If what's happening is less of a safety issue and more of a discomforting instance of how we're being perceived based on some identity or physical feature of ours, how might we "advocate for our rights" without coming off as an "Ugly American" or another type of insensitive Westerner?

- Our skin colors simultaneously say a lot about who we are, and at the same time, don't say enough. How might we find a sense of inner equanimity when people both at home and abroad are busy reacting to our first-impression outer package?

- -

Cluster 3: Homecomings, Kind Of

Going abroad to a place your parents or grandparents are from, or a place from where you've been adopted, or a place where, finally, you look more like the local people than you usually do in the West, can feel incredible. To see yourself reflected in the faces and skin tones and hair all around you can affirm and root us in a longer history than we might have known.

Homecoming trips, though, can also be complex for a range of reasons. Who am I, we might ask ourselves. How do I think of me here, and how am I being read and why? Here are two stories that center the homecoming journey and their complexities, complexities that are reflected in the emotional crests and falls of the travelers, and the interaction between anticipation and reality.

> SENAIT: For my student Senait, who had been born in the United States, the daughter of Eritrean immigrants, her study abroad program to Ghana was to be a homecoming of sorts, her first opportunity to return to the African continent of her parents and ancestors. Ghana, in West Africa, is different than east Africa, but closer to her Eritrean roots than the suburb of Washington DC, where she'd been born and raised. She describes feeling as though her world has seemed split between the Eritrean diaspora community of her parents and the mostly white schools she's attended. In college, she's gravitated toward classes

that help explain her homeland and the African continent beyond the usual stereotypes of poverty and corruption. Will things *feel* different in Africa than they do in the United States, she wonders? What will it be like to be in all-Black space all the time? She is overwhelmed with possibility and apprehension.

Now, in Ghana's capital city of Accra, even though Senait is as Black as most Ghanaians, Ghanaians somehow know she is a foreigner, an American, an *obruni*, even though her skin looks like theirs. People are very friendly and welcoming, but she is not a daughter of the soil as she once hoped. Or rather, she is in some ways, but not as she had imagined. Her identities don't seem to fit together here the way they work at home. "In the US," she says, "I'm Black and African. Here, I am coming to terms with being seen as not African and more as an American. Here I am lumped in with rich and power-holding people from the West including whites, but in my everyday life in the US, I'm Black and African and clearly not as good as actual whites. When can I be Black, American, and African, all at the same time?"

NIYA: I meet Niya, a mixed-race Latina undergraduate, at a writing workshop. She tells me this story during lunch one day. It's a story that she's trying to write about, but it still feels too close. A few months before we met, Niya had participated in a study abroad program to Santo Domingo in the Dominican Republic (DR). Niya is one of three students of color on her program of twenty-five Americans from a large university. It's the first time she's traveled to Latin America. She's awash in the range of skin-colored Blackness: dark, light, medium, and everything in between, and it feels comforting, feels like home.

One night, the whole group goes out to a local bar. At the door, her classmates file in, but a bouncer bars her entry. "You cannot come in," he says in Spanish.

"Why not?" Niya responds in Spanish.

"Your hair," the bouncer says, pointing to her puffed up natural hair. His skin color is three shades darker than hers. "You cannot come in because of your hair. This is an upscale club."

Did he really just say that, she thinks? She's so shocked she cannot argue back or respond. Her bones wilt and she slinks away. Niya's two friends, also the only other students of color on the program, have heard the exchange and accompany her away from the club out of solidarity and a similar sense of injustice. They try to comfort her, but all of them now feel marked, less than, and on display, and all this in a country in which people look more like them than their white peers. The rest of the students, twenty-two of them, are already inside enjoying a night of drinking and dancing. For Niya and her two friends, however, the moment signifies a rupture, one that exacerbates the fault lines of race and what counts as beautiful and better. For the rest of program in DR, Niya lurks on the fringes of her white classmates. She stands back and lets others talk in class. She second-guesses her reception and presentation, and notes all the advertisements for skin lightening creams and hair straightening salons around the city. She mediates her experiences through her hair, her skin, her similarity and difference. Amidst the clamor of so many students, the program staff do not notice her withdrawal.

Holding Space Together

- Senait's deep desire to feel welcomed in Africa might seem like a big hope, but it's understandable when we think about the contemporary racialization of people of color, and specifically Black people, in the United States. Her experiences in Ghana, though, complicate her expectations of what Africa should feel like and thwart the neat resolution to her identity. Spend some time reflecting on the homecoming journey as its own kind of travel genre, one filled with yearning and expectation from deep within the soul. What makes us long for home? What makes us know we've found it? How might the concept of fluid and unfinished identities be useful for Senait and in other homecoming or homegoing journeys?
- If Senait's experiences resonate for you, how might you hold space for yourself, your desire for home, and your own longings? How might you learn to hold space as a classmate, colleague, or friend for Senait if what she's going through is totally unfamiliar to you?

- "Internalized oppression" refers to the harmful stereotypes and negative associations that the dominant group has believed about marginalized people, and now many marginalized people believe about ourselves. "Stay out of the sun, you'll get dark," is a directive that many people of color are told, not by white people but by other people of color who love us and want the best for us. It's an example of the ways that people of color have internalized the harmful concept that it's better and more advantageous to be light-skinned than dark-skinned. It's also an example of how we consciously and unconsciously police each other to fit into the dominant social norms, even if the norms are false, hurtful, and genetically impossible. Internalized oppression plays out not only in regards to race, but also with gender, sexuality, wealth, disability, and other identities and experiences.

  What is your familiarity with this concept? Have you consciously experienced this? Did you notice what was happening at the time? What did it feel like?

- How might internalized racism be playing out in the scene where Niya is denied entrance into the club? What are the broader ideas about race, social mobility, and beauty that are taking place in the bouncer's comment or, as referenced in Jasmine's story in cluster 2, in the ubiquitous advertisements that feature light-skinned models where the population is dark-skinned?

- Learning to love ourselves despite what we've been taught about us can be a painfully long and difficult process. These ideas can feel sensitive to talk about, especially if you are from a marginalized community and are recognizing how you might be harboring the same negative associations about people like you that have also hurt you in the past. How might we slowly and with care examine our beliefs and values, not just the conscious ones we can identify, but the unconscious ones we're unaware that we are wedded to? How can we stay open and stay brave when we're digging into unexplored territory?

- -

Cluster 4: Sweet Moments: Traveling Connections

Travel isn't only about discomfort and heartache. Based on who we are and the people around us, we can find truly special moments of connection across many different kinds of identities and experiences. This too is the power and promise of travel and crossing boundaries. We hope to connect and relate to others, however momentarily. When this happens, there's nothing quite like it. Here are four such short stories to bring us hope and ground us in gratefulness.

GRACE: A Korean-American student I've worked with before is one of two people of color among seventeen white students on her two-week service-learning program located in a small town in Argentina. "Yes, I stick out, but not necessarily in a bad way," says Grace. "The Argentinians I meet don't know many people who look like me. They are curious to know more, and come up to me and ask questions about my identity, about Asia and why I'm here. It took me a little while to get used to it, but now I kind of like it. Their curiosity is a nice ice-breaker, and helps me practice my Spanish way more than I would have otherwise. I feel like myself but also different. I'm proud of how outgoing I'm becoming, and am really enjoying my friendships with local people. I wonder what it will be like to be back home after this experience."

AMINA: Amina is a friend of mine, a Muslim woman born and raised in London. She thinks back to her experiences traveling in Turkey. "Wherever my friends and I went, I was seen by the Turkish people as 'one of them' because I was the Muslim in our group. Even though I am British and originally from Bangladesh, the Turkish people I met spoke so nicely to me. It felt great to be welcomed into a new country and culture like that. It sounds ideal, but it felt a little like we Muslims form community wherever we go based on our shared sense of identity even if culturally we come from different places. Last year," Amina continues, "I was on holiday in France and Belgium with my friends who are also British Muslim women. We quickly made friends with all the Black and Asian hotel workers. There was a sense of solidarity and friendly recognition that we were Global South people in the West. The workers all became our friends, and it felt like they watched out for us like family."

RAFAEL: A gay Chicano man on my study abroad program loves walking around the streets of South India. "Even though culturally I'm an outsider," he says, "I feel more at home here than I thought I would. Everyone is some shade of brown like me. It reminds me of being in Mexico, but it's also different. In the US I'm always one of a handful of brown people in a class, a restaurant, or on a road. Sometimes I'm the only one. Here, I like being in a sea of brownness." He pivots his gaze to a group of men sitting on the steps of a building with their hands companionably resting on each other's shoulders. "I also love that many men here are affectionate with each other in a way you just don't see in the US. They sit close together and hold hands in a friendly and culturally approved way. I know that most of these men aren't necessarily gay, but just being a part of their warmth and physical ease with one another relaxes and acknowledges something deep about me. Being here makes me feel whole."

ANU: My family and I are in Beijing, China, as tourists for a week. We spend our days visiting the city's main attractions, and today we've come to Tiananmen Square. Wide open concrete is flanked by national monuments and looming posters of Chairman Mao Zedong. Here, like most of the places we have visited, the brownness of my family flags us as easy-to-spot foreigners in the ubiquitous crowds of Chinese people all around. There must be what, two or three thousand people in this square alone, I think. Politely curious, people nearby glance at us. Sometimes they stare. If anyone catches my eye, I smile and slightly bow my head in what I hope is seen as a respectful greeting.

One elderly man stands at attention near me. He sports a tan tweed jacket that hangs low. His bow-kneed legs are encased in blue vinyl exercise pants, the kind that I imagine goes "swish-swish" with each vigorous step forward. Alas, the man is not as vigorous as his exercise pants promise, and he labors under his creaking bones toward me. He propels himself forward at an unhurried pace, and his slow gait make the vinyl sound more like "Sssswwwwiish. Pause. Sssswwwwiish." When he approaches me, he thrusts his hand out to shake mine. I lean back slightly, unsure how to respond. Do elders and younger people touch in casual greeting in China? As a woman, should I shake the hand of an elder man? I'm not familiar enough with the nuances of Chinese culture in regard to age, status, gender, and for-eignness, but quickly shift my bags from my right arm to left so I may return his handshake. His hand is worn and strong. The elder smooths down his jacket with the hand that is not holding mine. His face splits into a big and toothy grin, and I am a bit surprised he has so many teeth. He disengages his hand from mine, pats my shoulder and totters away. "Ssswwwwiish. Pause. Sssswwwiish."

As the hours pass, many more elders will approach me with outstretched hands. A few will whisper near my ear senti-ments I do not understand. Some elders touch my hand or arm and pat my shoulder. A few will grin a toothy or no-teeth smile. Some wave as they walk away. The Chinese elders' light touch on my skin feels good; they are gentle and kind and welcoming, and at least for a few moments, quell the feeling that I've harbored about how conspicuously dif-ferent I am from all those around me. Their handshakes and pats and whispers are small gestures in this big concrete square, and they include me among the thousands of peo-ple around us. Sometimes as an outsider it is wonderful to blend in. And sometimes, sticking out couldn't be sweeter.

- -

Holding Space Together

 • What kinds of special and unexpected moments have you experienced abroad or at home with strang-ers across identities and differences? How might moments like these stay within you and animate the memory of journeys long after you've come home?

- What would an honest sharing of different people's experiences look like in your life? What needs to happen for you to be more vulnerable about your discomforting feelings and share openly with others?
- What are ways we might practice silencing the judgement in our heads or pushing through the discomfort stinging our skin, and instead, offer one another the space to process our experiences out loud? What small things in our schools, work places, and communities might shift if more of us learned to value this kind of conversation and relationality?

Bringing It All Together

Heartfelt questions and mindful listening encourage us to feel seen and heard for who we are and help us make sense of all the confusing, aching, and delightful things we've experienced. You and I can't necessarily change how people react to us either when we're a block from our house, or when we're ten thousand miles away. What we can do, however, is to raise our awareness of how identities shapeshift and morph, and what that might feel like for different people at different moments and contexts.

Thinking about ourselves through society and history helps us better understand that we are always figuring out who we are based on our context, and always interacting with wider frames, wherever in the world we might be. With practice, we

- Notice what's happening and consider why this might be so
- Consider how concepts and histories of mythical norms, under-visibility, and hyper-visibility might be playing out

- Consider what kinds of structures of more-or-less advantage might be in operation
- Reflect on why this might be going on and what it means for people's lives

All this analyzing, though helpful, doesn't necessarily scrub the pain out of a painful situation or clear the confusion from a confusing experience. We'll still feel all that we feel. What these steps can do, though, is to offer us ways to slow down our process and adequately address the feelings and the broader social systems that influence them. With a bit more spaciousness, we might be able to better navigate our way back to a more grounded center. And when you really think about it, isn't this what we *all* are seeking, every one of us?

CHAPTER 6

Limits to the Well-Intentioned Desire to Do Good:
The Politics of Help

IF WE LINK GLOBAL CITIZENSHIP TO THE STAMPS IN OUR PASSPORT OR the ethnic flair that enhances our wardrobe, we keep our global engagement superficial and consumerist. One thing that limits our understanding of global citizenship is the assumption that history resides in the past and that the present is all that matters. To disrupt this initial tendency, we can learn to see our travels through a more conscientious and questioning gaze, a gaze that notes that history's scars have affected many of us and are peppered throughout the present-day relationships within countries and between different regions of the world. I was shaped by these histories, as were my companions on my trip to India as a college student and later in Morocco—we were all shaped by these histories. Same with the travelers you've heard from in the cluster stories who received differential treatment because of how they were perceived. All of us interact with the past in our present from the vantage point of our identities, advantages, and positionalities. The intertwined historical legacies of structural inequality, racism, slavery, colonialism, patriarchy, migration, conflict, and contemporary global hierarchies are the mostly hidden authorities we currently use to appraise and judge others, and in turn, how we are appraised and judged.

As a well-intentioned traveler, I might mean no harm, yet every time I travel, I enter a story of systemic opportunity and adversity that's been playing out long before me. No matter how justice-minded I might be, my journeys intersect with these historical legacies. Where

we go, who is able to enjoy which opportunity, who isn't, and who gets to go somewhere or nowhere are all part of this longer story. Today, very few Westerners go abroad to resuscitate the imperial past. Most of us would never knowingly do harm, yet despite our good intentions, old frameworks still structure the politics of our current global identities and the geographical routes of our travels.

Ironically, less wealthy countries of the Global South are attractive to many Global North travelers precisely because of Western histories of wealth extraction and current global inequalities. The cost of living is cheaper in many Global South countries than in the West, and Western travelers take advantage of this fact. The inexpensive and newly discovered places that beckon Western travelers reflect, to a great extent, the unequal political and economic relationships that originated under colonial and imperial rule. More young adults from the West are choosing to go to the Global South, partly because they are curious about these regions, and partly because these parts of the world are cheaper than Europe. It's good for us to ask ourselves why this is so. In her book *Questions of Travel: Postmodern Discourses of Displacement,* scholar Caren Kaplan explains the connection between contemporary traveling routes and the history of inequality:

> Imperialism has left its edifices and markers of itself the world over, and tourism seeks these markers out, whether they consist of actual monuments to field marshals or the altered economies of former colonies. Tourism arises out of the economic disasters of other countries that make them "affordable" or subject to "development," trading upon long established traditions of economic and cultural hegemony and, in turn, participating in new versions of hegemonic relationships.

Many of the Global North to Global South journeys that Western travelers engage in via study abroad, service learning, and global volunteer brigades even follow the well-worn routes forged out of colonial and imperial pasts between "the mother country" and "her colonies," routes that divided the world into ruler and ruled, more-resourced and less-resourced. Think Britain and India, Britain and Kenya, France and North Africa, Belgium and Congo, Portugal and Brazil, United States and the Philippines. Seen from a longer historical lens, travel is not as innocuous or celebratory as we might have once thought, even though we are encouraged to travel precisely to become global citizens. As Robert Gordon writes in his book *Going Abroad: Traveling Like an Anthropologist,* "Going abroad can have a whiff of neo-imperialism about it. . . . In the heyday of imperialism people traveled to the tropics to procure wealth in gold, ivory, or slaves. Nowadays they travel to acquire nature, sun, beaches, sex, and adventures. Travel reproduces in large part relations similar to those that imperialism did . . ."

It might feel distasteful to consider which global advantages shape our travels abroad, or uncomfortable to admit that our journeys have anything to do with the imperialism of yesteryears. Advantages are more difficult to notice and identify when we've had the privileges of enjoying them. Our good intentions, likewise, seem unassailable and critique-proof, often because they are coming from a good place.

That's Not Very Fair, Is It?

Urban cities can only tell you so much about India when about 67 percent of the country's population is categorized as rural.

I am with a group of undergraduate students, and we leave the traffic and construction of big city life to visit my friend and colleague Mr. Mallesh's native village in a lush area of the state of Karnataka. We arrive in the schoolyard where Mallesh knows many of the school teachers and staff members. He chats amicably with everyone. He introduces my group as "students from Amreeka," and draws me forward to meet the principal and teachers. "Hello Madam," they say in English before switching to Kannada.

While we exchange pleasantries, one hundred or so schoolchildren crowd the wooden doorway, hoping for a glimpse of the foreigners who have come to visit. The kids make a collective blur of brown skin encased in both dark and light blue school uniforms. Their black hair is neatly arranged into obedience, cropped short for all the boys, cropped short or kept long in braids for the girls. They giggle when we make eye contact with them, just like my students giggle when the kids make eye contact with us. I honestly cannot tell who seems shyer, my students or these schoolchildren.

"May we speak directly to a few children?" we ask the principal. "Perhaps they too might have questions for us." A teacher heads toward the mass of blue uniforms and selects the school's brightest stars, three boys and two girls, all around the age of ten or eleven. He positions them in front of us in a cluster of achievement.

"What is your name? Which grade are you in? What is your favorite subject? Are you doing well in school?" My students ask polite questions in English. Mallesh and I translate into Kannada.

The children respond and ask equally polite questions in return: "How long are you in India? Do you like our village?"

One of the girls advances forward, legs ashy beneath her skirt, face scrubbed bright. Her braid is oiled like a shiny snake dangling from her head. She stands underneath a fan that creaks the air from one side to another like a swing. Eyes aglow, this child's got oodles of spunk and drive. "You all are from America, yes?" We nod.

"Do you have questions for us?" I ask. I imagine she will ask my students if they like India, if they like Indian food, what is their favorite dish. This is what most children ask.

Instead, the child says, with no preamble, no chitchat about food: "Since you have come from America, please explain this: Why is India poor compared to America and Britain and other countries? Why is there less opportunity here in India?" This young girl, days out of childhood, roots herself in front of our foreign delegation like a practiced reporter. I blink in amazement, and she further probes. "Why do so many Indians migrate and go abroad to work in America? Americans are not forced to migrate and come to work in India in the same way, isn't that so?"

She pauses for breath. Her arms relax, and my mind whirrs like the fan's blades. Damn, I think. This kid asks good questions. Her razor-sharp understanding of global economics is So Right On!

"Please tell me," she continues, "who decided that one US dollar is equal to sixty Indian rupees? It must have been an American. How come an Indian didn't get to decide that one Indian rupee equals sixty US dollars instead?" By now I'm not shocked by her questions, and find myself nodding in agreement.

She closes with the observation, "India is not equal to America. That's not very fair, is it?"

I finish translating the last few sentences from Kannada to English for my students. They too blink their surprise at the elegance of her questions, the simplicity of her logic. The girl is now quiet, and the air around us hums with life.

Surface Platitudes vs Deep Honesty

Truth has a way of chop-chopping through brambles of bullshit, those platitudes that celebrate how "we are all the same" and "everybody has a fair shot at everything." Actually: no. My students and I are from the place that is so clearly on the receiving end of global advantages. Our favorable dollar-to-rupee conversion rate is based on the rupee-to-dollar unfavorability. None of us in that schoolhouse under that whirling fan did anything to make things the way they are, but the growing realization that one group's advantages are directly linked to another group's disadvantage feels—yes, honest, but also uncomfortable. This isn't just theoretical anymore. The schoolchildren and us: we are the specifics of the theory that proves who has more access, who has more or fewer chances to enjoy more advantages on the global stage.

One of my students asks the young girl if she'd like to go to America to study or work. "Would you like to follow in the footsteps of the many Indians who have migrated to the West over the last few decades? There are many Indians in Seattle," the student adds helpfully.

It's not a surprising question, for many Indians have oriented themselves to the West to pursue work, graduate studies, or professional advancement. In the early 1960s, my father too was part of this trajectory. He left his hometown of Mysore, first for England, and eventually settled in the United States with my mother. Something about my students' question about migration makes me feel heavy, like I should be slouching. The girl with the slick braid, though, stands tall among us. She appraises our group and takes a moment to formulate her response to my student's question.

"No," she says, "I want to be in India. I want to be able to live a good life here. Tell me, why must I come to your country to live a good life?"

Her fortitude to stay in India and forge a good life for herself sounds strong and wonderful. Why indeed should this young girl be beholden to the West or any other region of the world? A just and equitable global landscape would offer her everything she needed right in her own country; all possibilities for advancement, education, dignity, and opportunity would be available everywhere and not just in pockets of geographies elsewhere.

I'm impressed by the girl's analysis and applaud her commitment to stay in her country. I'm also realizing that the slouchy feeling that increasingly enervates my limbs is because I feel personally implicated by her comments. She's obviously not talking about me, nor does she seem to judge me, but I can't help but see my own story through her strong convictions. I am, right in front of her, the literal product of people who left their homeland. My parents left India decades ago and made a life for themselves in the Global North. Does this mean they did not have the fortitude to stay and make a good life for themselves in India like the girl with the braid insists should be possible? I know from the stories of my family and many other immigrants that fortitude looks different in different contexts. People work hard in many different ways, and comparing across contexts isn't so precise or helpful.

And yet, what the girl says is also quite right. People from around the world should not have to orient themselves to a Global North country for opportunity, exciting prospects, and a better standard of living. I absolutely believe that ideally, people should be able to make choices not based on the colonial and imperial histories—and current economic and military policies—that have amassed wealth and prosperity in some pockets of the world while impoverishing others. These historical scars, of course, matter to us because they continue to play out in the present. Though we live in postcolonial times, many scholars contend that we have not fully transcended the colonial since Western influence on the Global South continues up until today. The West not only influences what happens in other parts of the world, but actively orchestrates certain affairs. While rural India or DR Congo or El Salvador or Rwanda can hoist a new flag on the dawn of independence and sing a new national anthem, too many areas of the Global South remain locked into unequal relationships born of colonial histories with the Global North.

The girl's comments cleanly state the privileges of Global North opportunity from the vantage point of a Global South perspective. Rural India or DR Congo or El Salvador or Rwanda can rarely offer the same glittery promises that gleam brightly from the United States, Canada, and New Zealand: everybody knows this. To me, it feels at once lucky and odd and reprehensible to be from the place that gleams brighter than other places. How does this happen? What systems need to be in place for my students and me to be here in a small rural school in the Indian countryside grappling with our guilt and privilege, and not the other way around?

The girl's comments about staying and my unsettledness about my family's leaving also underscore for me how travel can never be innocuous. When we travel—whether as immigrants, study abroad students, or anyone, really—all of us ride on the waves of global advantage and disadvantage. This historically inflected contemporary inequality is the context and backdrop we travel through as we journey from the Global North to the Global South. We journey abroad for different reasons and in different ways with different consequences and experiences—but some of us are given a paddle to help navigate those waves we ride; some of us aren't. That's not very fair, is it?

The West and the Rest, More and Less

When I consider why the girl with the braid or the other schoolchildren we met that afternoon might have different opportunities than my students and I, I think about the "West and the Rest" categories and the "more" and "less" descriptors we use to describe countries:

- More development and infrastructure = more resources = more opportunities for more of us.
- Less development and infrastructure = less resources = less opportunity for more of us.

These more-or-less indicators translate to actual outcomes for real people and communities. They affect people's lives in both small and big ways. In the Global South, the visual signs of less wealth and fewer resources are on display. Roads might be bumpier with less paving. Vital resources may be scarce in many communities, with poverty more acute, forcing people to hustle in creative and sometimes taxing ways to bring food for their families. Government accountability can be questionable, and there are fewer social services available to middle-income and poor people. I'm making huge generalizations of course, and all the issues I've listed occur in less funded, economically challenged parts of Global North communities too. These issues can exist anywhere, but don't exist perhaps to the same degree everywhere.

Many regions of the Global South remain the Global South because of the persistence, degree, and historical roots of global inequality and difference. We can even say that many regions of the Global South are kept in place by a current global economic order that has been forged from the past, and remains in place through various processes of Western-dominated trade, economic regulations, militarism, and cultural hegemony. What makes these issues all the more complex is that many of us in the West have learned very little about how most parts of the world have been, as postcolonial scholar Gayatri Chakravorty Spivak says, "worlded" through these historical and current processes.

All these visible and invisible forces affect how we journey from the Global North to the Global South, what we struggle with or what we imagine as exciting or novel. Our media, books, art, and pop culture all work together to reinforce our ideas about other places, and teach us which country on the other side of the planet, or much closer still, which area of town, is more-or-less than another. Oftentimes, even before we board a plane to go elsewhere, our preconceived ideas of the more-or-less of other places have already been formed.

- -

Holding Space Together

- Think back to Audre Lorde's mythical norm, describing the relationship between advantage and disadvantage on a personal level. The closer we are to the mythical norm, the more advantage we experience and the further away, the more disadvantage. Being far away from the center of power also means we are more likely to be conscious of the mythical norm's power and it is more likely we might agitate for change. How is this illustrated in the story of the girl with the braid? What's the connection between the more-or-less of human identities, power, and hierarchy and the more-or-less of country identities, power, and hierarchy?

- Think about the various labels people put on different parts of the world via the terms Third World, Global North, Global South, developing country, developed, and so on. How might this affect the ways we imagine who "we" are and who "others" are, especially if we come from a "more" country? What might it mean for our national or regional identity if we come from a "less" country?

- In Salman Rushdie's novel *Midnight's Children,* narrator Saleem Sinai states that, "To understand just one life, you have to swallow the world. I told you that." This quote nicely demonstrates the interconnections each of us have to the broader sweeps of history, change, conflict, and human movement. To better understand your life and the lives of members of your family and community and the lives of your ancestors, how might you need to "swallow the world"? What would that entail?

Going Abroad as a Friend

Our history belongs to all of us, but we are all differently positioned by it depending on who we are, where we come from, how we identify and are seen by others. The good news is that neither you nor I made the world the way it is today. We are not directly responsible for the systematic impoverishment of parts of the Global South—and some areas of the Global North—over the last few centuries or in our present moment. The bad news, though, is that history has everything to do with me, and it has everything to do with you. In fact, many of us in the Global North and in wealthy pockets of the Global South continue to enjoy benefits from this unequal history.

"I don't want to be seen as an imperial sahib," Evan, a twenty-something British traveler in India, tells me over tea. He uses the term sahib, the local Indian term for "sir" that was used to refer to the British during colonial times. "I am a white person from London, for sure. I see how the history of colonialism offered me and my family advantages that other people throughout the world have not received. I try not to come off as a spoiled sahib who uses the natives for my own pleasure and fun. I'm here in India as a friend to all. But how do I actually convey this?"

What a spot-on question. As travelers, we might find ourselves in a quandary, not wanting to unwittingly rehearse the unequal dynamics of the past that have given rise to our unequal present. But this is bigger than you or me as individual travelers, and bigger than Evan or the Indian schoolgirl with the braid. The enormity of the problems, of course, is what often confounds our emotions as we leave our relatively "more-than" contexts to travel to regions that might be "less-than" in different ways, and find ourselves interacting with people across these divides and different realities. These global histories of disadvantage and advantage differentially manifest in our present, and plunge us into the icy recognition that we have more, look different, or represent wealth. Most of all, noticing our identities and differences can help us think through our values and ask: What kind of society do we want to seed and see bloom before us? Who should matter more than another?

Doctor, activist, and writer Paul Farmer has said, "The idea that some lives matter less is the root of all that is wrong with the world." He's right. From the stigma attached to people with HIV to everyday police profiling, the hyper-sexualization of women's bodies to the power to make war: all these instances tell the story of some group that has the power to define the reality for another group. These bigger stories then merge with and shape our own smaller stories so that we are, in effect, "swallowing the world" to understand our lives. Often, we know little about the stories of people who are not like us. Not knowing each other's stories—especially in such an unequal world—has dire consequences in terms of people's health, opportunities, and life paths. "I have come to believe," says Sriram Shamasunder, an American doctor who works in global health, "that needless deaths, deaths from treatable illnesses, start when narratives go unheard. Whose suffering matters less, and why?" The more-or-less-ness of our world, indeed, matters greatly. When we cultivate a culture of curiosity to wonder why people like us aren't on our screens or why some lives seem to matter less than others, perhaps we can begin to unpack the histories of unfairness and hierarchies that persist today.

If we don't want to go abroad and inadvertently act like a colonial sahib, we need to pay close attention to our own positionality, as well as better understand how history and structures of power play out in other people's lives during our travels. This is sometimes difficult to do as an outsider coming in with different lenses, especially when local hosts may want to leave you with a good impression of their country instead of airing their "dirty laundry."

Whenever I've traveled to new places, I often ask my local friends about power structures in their communities and cultures. Which groups feel they are better (or more powerful or more authentic or belong more than another) and why? How are boundaries between groups explicitly policed and implicitly disciplined to ensure group separation? Or might boundaries between different groups be more fluid and situational? How did this superiority play out in the past, and what's changed in its contemporary manifestations? Depending on the local cultural norms and with whom I'm speaking, I might not be able to ask these questions so directly. In other ways then, I try to dig below the surface a bit surreptitiously.

My friends' responses to these issues, along with the strong feelings they inspire, have helped me better understand the dynamics of apartheid and contemporary racism and classism in South Africa, French colonialism in West Africa and the contemporary scramble of Europeans purchasing West Africa's prime real estate, the links between the feudalism of yesteryears and contemporary globalization in South Asia, and neocolonial privatization in Mexico in relation to the US demonization of the border. These conversations help ground my understanding of how histories of "the West and the Rest" manifest in people's day to day lives, not just from my outsider lens but from the perspective of local people who are both invested in and resistant to these social structures. Such questions can be critically useful as we learn to see our traveling contexts from many angles and attempt to better understand our home contexts.

Pills and Pads

"Go abroad while making a difference!" the advertisement beckons. That's what Viet, the young man in my office, has desired for the past year. He's a former student and someone I know quite well. Now, he sits in my office. "Sits" is perhaps too aspirational a verb, for rather he sags and slumps and spills over the wooden furniture. What a marked contrast to his energy just two months ago, I think. Then he had run into my office, gushing excitement like a high-spirited fountain. He was about to go abroad to a village three hours outside of Lima, Peru, and the pre-med mission trip was just the opportunity Viet had been searching for to marry his love of travel and passion for medical justice. I knew of his earnestness and genuine commitment to support medical care for people in low-resource countries. Perhaps, I hoped, he might have finally experienced a concrete application of the ideas he had been learning about for the last two years. Now, a few weeks back home after his trip, his story of deflation emerges.

"We got to Lima on a Sunday evening and drove straight to the village. By next morning we volunteers were ready to go and looking good in new t-shirts. We were so excited! Finally, we thought, here was our chance to contribute to the health care of folks who really needed it. And then we got to the health camp." Viet's enthusiasm dries into silence, face closed, eyes dim.

"So what happened?" I prod.

"This is the health camp I was telling you about before I went, the health camp that receives funding from some of the biggest players in global health."

"Yes, I remember our discussion a few months ago. How did you all help the community?"

Viet scoffs. "Help? I'm not sure we helped anybody there, really. All we did was hand out bottles of pain relievers to the village men and sanitary pads to the women." Viet pauses, and fiddles with the zipper on his backpack. "I spent $3000 and went all the way to a village in Peru to supply Tylenol and Kotex to villagers."

I'm confused with the account. I had thought health camps were medical hubs of sorts, remote and sometimes makeshift clinics that for a set amount of time, brought together doctors, nurses, physician assistants, and community health workers from around the community and around the world to offer targeted medical assistance to the community. "I don't get it," I say. "I thought you all were going to volunteer at the health camp for ten days. Weren't you supposed to learn how to do stuff and gain some kind of experience in the health field?"

"And we did, I guess," Viet says, "I learned a bit about global health, but not much. We typed up a report or two, but mostly we smiled and just hung around. The whole trip felt really weird to me," he replies. "I'm not quite sure why we were there. I mean, the villagers definitely need better health care, but we never quite understood what their situation was or what their lives were like. We also never really talked about the health camp and what we were supposed to be doing. We were there for ten days and seemed to just take up space. The organizers had told us we had something very valuable to offer this village, but I'm not sure what that was." Viet and I are quiet for a few moments, and I'm not sure how to respond.

Finally, he leaks a long sigh. "I've worked hard to get into pre-med and do well in my classes. I want to be a doctor who works with low-resource communities abroad. Or at least, I thought so before this trip. Tell me, what were we doing in Peru besides looking cute in our matching t-shirts?"

Business-as-Usual vs Something Ethical: Decolonizing

Viet and his classmates figured that since they enjoyed more resources and opportunities for good health than others, they should help. Many of us are passionate about our travels abroad because we care for others and want to assist communities in need. We realize we have more than others, and want to help and make a difference as a friend, especially through global partnerships that connect institutions and people across resources and geography. And yet we need to seriously consider: are we ever able to bypass the structural inequalities and historical contexts within which these global partnerships arise and that have socialized our understanding of the word "help" in the first place?

Scholars Ron Krabill and Benjamin Gardner critically investigate the term "global partnership," a term that "implies a kind of equality in agency if not in resources." They write, "The frequent mobilization of the term—particularly in connection to the African continent—seeks to convey that the individuals or institutions involved in those partnerships have moved beyond the inequitable relationships of the past: slavery, colonialism, structural adjustment, Cold War military domination, and cultural imperialism. According to the discourses of global partnership, our relationships are no longer ones of exploitation or domination—in short, neo-colonialism—but rather ones of reciprocity and mutual benefit. We call bullshit."

So, let's ask the pointed questions—How *do* we do our work within a historically unequal global context? How do we pay close attention to things we'd rather sweep under the (very heavy) rug of our good intentions? Viet's story brings to mind many questions: what are the global politics of our partnerships and collaborations? Are there ways to build better connections across mammoth power differentials without reinforcing the inequality and advantages in the social equation? Without conscientious and frequent discussion about the dynamics of history, identity, and systems of power embedded in any partnership—global or domestic—partnerships run the risk of concealing the inequitable dynamics at play while prematurely celebrating and romanticizing reciprocity.

Though Viet and his classmates surely know their short-term medical service trip cannot solve all the Peruvian villagers' issues, they do hope to lighten the villagers' suffering on a small scale. This is a laudable and beautiful goal. Medical service trips as well as a variety of developmental, environmental, educational, humanitarian, or disaster-relief initiatives might be based upon the spirit of help and aid, but even when they are considered a success, they are often able to only address the symptoms. The broader inequities in health and access to resources require much more radical and systemic solutions at both the national and international level. Short-term, "band-aid" approaches to help, care, and aid cannot, by definition, adequately address the complicated factors involved in the historic inequalities that differentially manifest in our present. (There is, though, an important pedagogical role for short-term trips. Such trips have the potential to sensitize and expose us to the issues and contexts that different people face in different parts of our world.)

We need to look carefully at not only the global relations within which our desires to help are located, but also our own selves. Our place as advantaged Westerners (of any color and race) complicates the terrain of global partnerships and the politics of help. As Ivan Illich's famous piece "To Hell with Good Intentions" argues, "Next to money and guns, the third largest North American export is the U.S. idealist, who turns up in every theater of the world: the teacher, the volunteer, the missionary, the community organizer, the economic developer, and the vacationing do-gooders. Ideally, these people define their role as service. Actually, they frequently wind up alleviating the damage done by money and weapons, or 'seducing' the 'underdeveloped' to the benefits of the world of affluence and achievement." Though Illich wrote these words in 1968, his razor-sharp appraisal remains valid and applicable more than ever.

The Western volunteering industry has been widely critiqued as a naive avenue for Westerners to feel accomplished without having to engage with the structural issues from which they benefit, all the while posing as the saviors of struggling less-developed locals who are stereotypically portrayed as passive, helpless, and pitiable. (If that last sentence makes you cringe, please do read it again.) And while we do need to call bullshit on over-romanticized notions of help that mask the unfair power dynamics at play, we will lose a valuable resource if we downplay goodness and ignore the desire of many to help. Many of us hope to use our multiple advantages and access to resources to share what we often take for granted in our Western contexts and offer more opportunity and access to people with less. I'm not sure how to reconcile all these conflicting and confounding ideas solely on my own. I do know that we make a dent when together we first acknowledge the existence of such tensions and channel our energy into critical questions and deep reflections.

These discussions aren't about being bad or good people. There are many of us who engage in admirable work abroad. We are passionately engaged in the communities we've entered, and think carefully about access, accountability, responsibility, collaboration, and the politics of our ethics and good intentions. And yet, even when we're doing good work, none of us can remain outside the broader structures that have given rise to the inequalities we are trying to address. Anytime we are working within the field of structural inequality and working in a do-good capacity, we need to engage in explicit and repeated conversations about unequal power, identity, difference, and history. Without such essential conversations and many questions along the way, students like Viet remain unsettled. How much more effective would it have been for this frustrated young man and his classmates to talk openly about what they saw and experienced instead of merely stating, "Great job, now you're a global citizen! Please pose for another photo."

In the words of Anna, a global health graduate student I worked with recently, "I think talking about what many of us are—white American students with relative class and education privilege who work in Global South countries—is so important to the field of global health. We should be asking ourselves hard questions before we go into the field, during our time abroad, and after we come back. The discussion about identity, history, and power," she said, "should very well be the core of our curriculum." Though not all of us are white Americans like Anna, I think we can still relate to her comment. All of us indeed navigate our own identities and advantages, a global history of inequity, and differential power structures that rank us differently in different moments. Critical self-awareness and a handful of good questions help take our good intentions further. While there is no silver bullet and talk on its own can't resolve everything, our honest

discussions can, at least, begin the process of grappling with how history's legacies often continue into the present, how we feel about it, and what we choose to do about it.

When we boldly acknowledge and learn about this historic baggage, we can then repack our contemporary loads and journeys with more care. As John Willinsky writes in *Learning to Divide the World: Education at Empire's End*, "We need to learn again how five centuries of studying, classifying, and ordering produced enduring and powerful ideas of race, culture, and nation that were, in effect, concepts that the West used both to divide up and educate the world." For many of us, learning is a simultaneous process of unlearning and relearning:

- We unlearn the status quo that offers more of many things to fewer of us and relearn how to pay close attention to different people's lived experience.
- We unlearn the myths of the norm to relearn more truths of more of us.

If we ignore history or history's impact on our present identities and imagine that we are individuals freed from the past, we simply replay a colonial gesture. If, by contrast, we share our experiences of how the connections between past and present affect our travels and how we are situated within systems of opportunity and adversity, we begin to reflect a decolonizing stance. You can decide what kind of traveler you want to be.

Holding Space Together

- How does our desire to appear altruistic, generous, and selfless affect our motivation to help others? Is it possible to help others without any expectation for ourselves?
- What part of helping and serving is focused on ourselves, and what part of helping and serving is focused on the ones receiving assistance?
- Why might helping people who live far away feel different than helping people closer to home? What kind of weight or importance is placed on "the going" somewhere far to help?
- What are the identities of people who usually go far to help? What are their identities in relation to our mythical norm and its margins?
- Why do you think the villagers in Peru that Viet and his classmates travel to might be in need of assistance? Why might it be problematic or inadequate for Viet and the others on his program to distribute the pills and pads to the villagers? Why, conversely, might distributing the supplies be perfectly alright?
- What is your opinion on the scholars quoted earlier "calling bullshit" on some global partnerships? What might reciprocal collaboration and global partnership with communities in different countries look and feel like, not just for Viet and his global health classmates, but for the receiving community too? How would we know if and when our partnerships are truly ethical and just?
- How much of this past is really our responsibility? Who should be accountable for the painful, unequal past and the painful, unequal present?

The Incense Spinner: What Do We Do with What We Know?

I am with a group of US students in a peri-urban area in India out-side of a large metropolitan city. We meander through a small village, stopping to chat with residents along the way to learn about liveli-hood issues in this community that straddles the urban and rural. Ms. Indhu and Ms. Usha serve as our guides and coordinators for the day. They are long-time feminist organizers, activists, and researchers in India who I've been partnering with for years. Indhu and Usha wave our group over. We see a young woman sitting and working on her veranda, the open-air porch of her home. She must be in her early twenties or so. The woman's palms are blackened. She spins her palms quickly together over a twig, applying a paste that will trans-form the wispy stick into fragrant incense. We circle in to watch her. She throws a quick glance our way and simply continues to work, composed and unruffled by our presence. Her movements are precise, and she speedily flicks stick after stick between her stained hands. Her two young children play nearby, and a dog lounges comfortably against her right leg.

Indhu and Usha greet and speak with the woman in Kannada, and I translate for the students. They ask her about her work, the black-ened palms, the twigs she spins. We learn that in addition to her house-work and farm work, the woman rolls incense 2–3 hours a day for the extra daily income of Rs.60, approximately $1.00. It's a fairly good situation, she tells Indhu. We learn that her name is Lavanya, and she is twenty-four years old. "It's good because I can be with my children and still work. Otherwise, who will look after them all day if I work in a factory?" The older child looks up at her. He's probably four, and his little sister on the cusp of two.

One of my students asks to take a picture of the family by ges-turing at her camera; the lady smiles shyly. She seems amused that a group of foreigners find her photo-worthy. Usha explains that we are students who have come to learn about different people in India, and even though we might use incense in our homes far away, most of us have never seen it being made. Waggling her head sideways, Lavanya gives my student permission for the photo. The camera clicks, momentarily stilling the blur of her hands and sticks.

Home Work: Flexibility and Exploitation

Incense—in Kannada known as *agarbatti*—enjoys ubiquitous use from the medical to the religious throughout South Asia. Agarbatti also perfumes the subcontinent and its global market with big business and big profits. As one of the most labor-intensive of traditional industries in India, agarbatti can be spun and rolled in the "comforts and convenience" of home, making it a diffuse and highly unregulated enterprise. The state of Karnataka in South India leads in this industry with main production manufacturing centers in Mysore, Bangalore, and surrounding areas. More than a thousand such centers exist through the state, employing hundreds of thousands of rural and low-skilled people like the woman we've just met.

"Home work" industries like agarbatti are notoriously tricky to pin down to global ethical standards and workers' rights. In unregulated and informal industries with lax rules and little oversight, managers and those in the middle might very well exploit their workers. And yet, the very unregulated-ness and flexibility of the industry make it possible for Lavanya and millions of agarbatti spinners around the region to earn extra income while caring for family.

Is it Too Much to Ask?

The small kids now scamper on their mother's lap. Lavanya gently pushes them off with her elbow, careful to not stain the children with the resin on her hands. She picks up another twig to spin. Lavanya tells us that the middleman from the factory collects her handmade incense sticks once a week and pays her. She and her husband are both from a nearby village, one that is smaller with less amenities and opportunity. Not able to cultivate their family's lands anymore because of development and drought, they migrated to the city where her husband now drives an auto rickshaw. Her mother also lives with them, as well as frequently visiting relatives from the village who are also seeking new opportunities. Lavanya tells us that by God's grace, her family's frugality, hard work, and meager earnings secure their small rental home and just enough food to eat.

We thank Lavanya the agarbatti spinner for her time and bid her family goodbye. The older child waves happily, and his young sister half-pets, half-pulls the hair of the dog who continues to lie placidly alongside the mother. Her story of hard-earned income hangs in the air as we exit the village and gather under the illustrious shade of a majestic banyan tree. Indhu signals us into a close huddle. "There's another layer to the agarbatti industry that you should know about, a layer that directly impacts the workers' health. The workers coat the twigs into incense sticks with a resin that is quite dangerous. It's most likely carcinogenic. Most of the workers in this industry know little about the various chemicals that penetrate their skin and travel through their bloodstream. The lady we just met probably does not know of the cancer risks to herself or her family. For her, this is a good job that supplements her family's income." When she finishes speaking, the air is silent. The breeze blows along and amidst our huddle, and we continue to stand shoulder to shoulder. Carcinogenic?

Lavanya's blackened hands? We don't know how to incorporate this latest detail with the many complex stories we have been hearing during our program the last few weeks.

Throughout our time in India on my study abroad program, a wide range of local people have shared their struggles to access clean water, send their children to good schools, work for humane employers, and yield good crops. These people seek neither the sun nor the moon, but simple basic necessities: secure-paying jobs, decent medical facilities, and the dignity they deserve in dealing with municipal and governmental officials. How might working-class and urban poor communities not just survive but actually *thrive* in rapidly globalizing Global South economies that have become increasingly unequal? Could toxic chemicals one day flow—or already be flowing!—through hard-working Lavanya and the bodies of her children? For us at that moment, Lavanya's story—her name and face and spinning hands and little children leaning against her leg—crystallized into a portrait. She became a figure who stood in for countless others and one we could yoke our thoughts to. We'd been in this community but a few hours, and already Lavanya had gained our admiration. She navigated the very restricted opportunities available to her with dignity and strength, making her and her family's lives better. We had started to care about her and her family. We felt the heartbreak of the ordinariness of her desire to provide all that she can for her young family.

A few days later, my students and I meet for a long debrief session. We are confused and sad, and process together our emotions, the stories we've heard, and what ethical action for Lavanya and so many others might look like. We ask each other: could there really be no relief to the aching difficulty some people must face? What might be in store for Lavanya and her family? Shouldn't we do something? How might we help?

Holding Space Together

- It feels wrong that my students and I knew that Lavanya's work might cause her harm, especially if she herself did not have access to this information. What does responsibility and justice look like in this situation? Should one of our local partners, Indhu or Usha, tell Lavanya that her work might cause her or her family irreparable harm? Should one of us tell her?
- Let's say we decide to tell her. How might that conversation go? "Hello. Remember us? That big gaggle of foreigners in front of your veranda the other day? Well . . . turns out that the black goopy stuff you soak your hands in might make you and your babies real sick . . ."
- If Lavanya decides to give up the job and forfeit the extra income that her family has come to rely on, do we play any role in helping her find alternatives?
- For the most part, my group and I are well-intentioned outsiders who know very little about the context of Lavanya's life. In our desire to share the info with her and "do right by her," are we acting like narcissistic saviors imagining we know best because of our better access to information, health care, and global positionality? Why or why not? But also consider: In not sharing this critical info with Lavanya, do we deny her the agency to choose for herself whatever she feels is right?
- How might our do-good desires to help Lavanya and women like her connect with the story of Viet and his classmates' desires to help the villagers in Peru on their medical mission? What is similar about these situations, and what is different?

- Consider your own sense of justice and ethics. What would you have done if you were part of our group that day? Would you have asked your local guides to tell the woman spinning the agarbatti about the toxins and the possible cancer, and stuck around to help assist in the possible fallout? Or would you have kept the information to yourself?

I'm still not sure which option or action is right or most ethical. In our specific case, my students and I thought about Lavanya and her young family often, but did not visit them again. We were relieved of having to choose what we should say or do. Sometimes breathing through our uncomfortable feelings helps us stay present so we can hold space for the different people we meet on our journeys. In this case though, holding space for Lavanya's story was important but did not seem like enough. We became quite unhinged at the broader ethics of our travels, our knowledge, and inadequacies, and did not know what to do in the various "what if" scenarios we constructed. As people who believed in and felt passionate about a better life for more people, Lavanya's dignity, hard work, and loving care for her family stayed with us. So, too, did the social injustices she faces to eke out a living. We gratefully took Lavanya's personal story and wove it into our increasing understanding of Indian working-poor people's lives. We did not, I am very sorry to say, give back even an iota of anything to her. While it wasn't me who caused the blackening of Lavanya's hands, there is definitely something toxic about taking more than we give.

CHAPTER 7

- - - - - - - - - - - - - - - - - - - -

Displace Guilt, Center Dignity, and Breathe:
Strategies to Stay Present

OUR MORE ADVANTAGEOUS POSITION WITH RESPECT TO WEALTH, access, and opportunity will be assumed to be a fact by many of the people we meet and engage with abroad. The schoolgirl with the braid from the Indian village knew this to be incontrovertibly true. And all our research on global economics and histories of colonialism might not prevent the deep discomfort we feel when we meet people whose lives seem quite different than ours. This discomfort, too, is the story of our global travels.

Imagine what relatively everyday objects—a pair of sturdy shoes or a fancy water bottle—signal in an unequal world. What does it mean that I am here in this community, we might ask? Whoa, my life looks so different than the lives of the people I'm meeting. We ask ourselves: Should I even be here? Our guilt coats and paints us as "the lucky ones." We can easily shut down and short circuit.

As we notice the dynamics of identity and listen deeply to others' stories, questions and discomforts will naturally arise. It can, for example, feel wrong to learn and take more from a community than we can give back in return, exactly as my students and I experienced with Lavanya the incense spinner. As well-intentioned people, we might ask: Are we justice-minded enough? How do we show this?

How our differences and advantages can make us and the people we meet feel is illustrated in greater detail in the following collection of stories. The first two stories—fictional but quite real in the feelings and issues raised—illustrate how the guilt of having more and being different might trip up travelers in different ways. The third story offers a portrait based on one of my own travels of how we might develop more resilience and find our way through the guilt, shame, and discomfort that traveling in an unequal world often produces in us.

You Are Hyper-Visible and You Can't See

Slinking out of his Nairobi hostel, Liam wonders if today, finally, he will be able to pass through the front gate without attention. The wilted leaves of the plants sag under the Kenyan brightness; it is hot outside. This is his first time in another country. The khaki shorts and green shirt he wears had been purchased specifically for this trip. "Tropical Armor: wicks away heat and moisture to keep you cool!" declared the glossy advertisement. Not so, he thinks, the first of many let-downs. His skin, now unfamiliarly ripe, prickles with the humidity of his sweat.

Liam is a twenty-year-old white student from an American public university. He is now tired, tired of the differences that once seemed exotic and enticing. He reminds himself what motivated him to come. Another glossy advertisement, this time of smiling Black children's faces along with the invitation to adventure: "See the World! Study Abroad Next Semester in Kenya!" Curiosity piqued, he fell into the idea quite naturally. Many of his friends had also studied abroad in far-flung countries, countries whose geographical specificity he couldn't quite locate. His friends all returned with tall tales, suntans, and an accomplished air, like they were in a special global club. Yes, why not, he thought, as he filled out the surprisingly brief application.

Here in the actual Kenya—the Kenya of dusty roads, crowded roads, and many Black people everywhere—Liam's senses are confounded. He is used to being anonymous, doing whatever he wants whenever the time suits him and without much attention. Here, though, his white skin glows like a beacon on a foggy night. Street children and hawkers encircle him wherever he goes. Sometimes the kids want money. Other times, they just want some attention. He knows the kids mean no harm, but he can't help feeling hounded and pursued, a bit like big game. What's a well-intentioned Westerner like him to do? It's not his fault these people are poor, he knows, he rationalizes. Should he give money to the kids? How does he know if they really need it? Maybe they are scamming him? This relentless rehearsal of hands outstretched, faces expectant, and calls of "Brother! Brother!" dig into the young man's patience. "Leave me the hell alone!" he wants to shout, "At home I'm just a poor college student!"

It's not that he hasn't thought about race or class before this trip. He knows he is white and from the United States, and that means something about his life opportunities. He knows he has more than many others around the world. He thinks of himself as sensitive, generous, thoughtful. And yet, he is having a hard

time here. He feels a youngster's hand yank his shirt. Yesterday Liam gave some change to the young boys around him. Today, should he refuse? His insides churn strongly with irritation and suspicion, but outwardly, he slumps, defeated and confused. He wants to help, to give and be just, to be charitable. He sees himself as a friend of the poor, frequently offering panhandlers and homeless youth back in his big American city spare change or half his sandwich. Here, though, the jostle of people makes his eyes go blank and pulse quicken.

Liam stirs; he needs some space. He is gentle but determined as he launches himself shoulder-first into the crowd that rings him. The circle breaks. He is now free, alone, not surrounded by children anymore. Now he gathers speed and distances himself from the crowd of hands, eyes, and bodies. His triumph mingles with disgrace, and his mouth feels chalky and metallic. Is this what shame tastes like, he wonders? This morning he had woken refreshed and ready. He had woken with the kind of wanderlust that celebrates the promise of travel, his own initiative, and the benefits of journeying across the seas. But now, severed from the human ring around him and standing by himself on this dusty road in Kenya, the thought of navigating and negotiating all that there is to navigate and negotiate wears him out. He is tired, and tired of being seen. He would rather be far away from the crowds, the hawkers with cheap plastic items for sale, the glossy advertisements, his white beacon, his guilt.

His sturdy sandals propel him down the road. There is a pub where expats and other foreigners like him flock, preen, gather, and consolidate themselves. The air inside cools his moistness, softens his irritation. On the walls of the pub, an artist has affected a safari complete with spots, manes, and hoofs. The comfortingly dark interior wicks away both the young man's worry and dust. Liam knows that just two frosty bottles of Tusker Premium Lager will dull his frustrations and steady his mood.

It's Just You and the Folks Who Watch You

Let's say it's mid-afternoon, and you are tired and hot and lonely. For the past three weeks you have lived in Accra, Ghana, interning at an NGO that focuses on women's rights. The sun warms your skull. Today is a holiday, and you will take a walk toward the sea. You hope to feel the freshness of the water cascade on your overheated toes, and to splash away your homesickness.

Or maybe you've been studying in Mumbai, India, and today you and your fellow study abroad classmates stride out of the hostel doors. Within seconds, your group quickly becomes a spectacle. You decide to bid your friends goodbye, and begin a long walk to Dadar, the busy railway station. More than half a million people zip in and out of Dadar station every day, and you're on your way to take a peek! It's nice to feel somewhat alone in this crowded city, you think to yourself as you happily bump shoulders with local people on their way to somewhere.

Or perhaps you might even be in Kingston, Jamaica, volunteering for two weeks at an orphanage as part of your voluntourism trip. You've had a great time playing with all the cute children, and today's your day off. You decide to visit Coronation Market, the famous gathering place, which bustles and throbs with colorful energy. You politely tell your homestay family father, "No thank you, a cab is not needed," and feel proud that he raises his eyebrows in surprise. You feel eager, brave, engaged, and want to get to know the city on your own terms.

Ghana, India, or Jamaica: where you are is not important, not because each location is somehow irrelevant or generic or feature-less or replaceable. Rather, it does not matter where you are because right now, you are a wealthy Global Northerner traveling through a more impoverished area of the Global South. Of course, you don't feel wealthy all the time. In Ghana, India, and Jamaica alike, all areas are not poor, and rich Ghanaian, Indian, and Jamaican people, come to think of it, are much richer than you. But today as you begin your personal excursion to the beach, railway station, or market, you find yourself in a much less wealthy area of the city. You're now, indeed, in a shantytown, an area that makes you start to feel wealthier than you usually feel.

Your feet step on and your body propels forward. Your eyes, though, stay locked in place: big-big eyes taking in information you haven't seen or had to process before. Local residents watch the foreigner who is you walk through their community. The people to your left and right live on and around the small path that snakes through the community of urban poor residents. Life—in all its mundane and pungent messiness—spills out every which way. Women outside their corrugated tin homes squat every few feet and fan coal stoves. Children play in stagnant pools of water. Everyone watches you, curious, because you are here, and people like you are usually not. What a novelty you are, this spectacle of one! The big children vibrate energy and shout "Hallo Hallo!" to you. The small children cling to the nearest adult's leg or arm. Some adults look upon you somewhat dispassionately. Some smile shyly. "What you are doing here?" is the question folks seem to be asking.

Urban slums, you have read, are the fastest growing human habitat across the planet. Over half of all people in Global South cities live in urban slums characterized by makeshift homes, irregular and inaccessible water, and poor sanitation. In a college class, you learned that urban slums are an unmistakable feature of Global South cities whose boundaries and resources stretch and press and snap at the seams. You've heard that most urban slums around the world are growing. And now, here you are.

The residents whose community you pass through know very well you do not belong here. This isn't about race, or rather, it's not only about race. Whether you are white, Black, brown, Asian, none of the above, or a combination of all of the above, your awkward gait, outsiderness, expensive backpack and water bottle state your Global North origins. Everyone knows you come from—and will ultimately return back to—somewhere else. Race, today, seems secondary to class and wealth and opportunity and passports. The fact that your shoes are this sturdy, and the fact that your eyes flit and fall as you glance at the children playing in puddles, makes what you have—or have access to—matter differently than the color of your skin, at least right now. Economics and global position are key, and you've got the right combo that—bingo!—unlocks the safe. You who have come to Ghana or India or Jamaica—or Bangladesh or Gambia or Mozambique or Brazil—have more compared to the urban poor community you walk through. And having more matters more, or perhaps more accurately, matters differently than your race right now.

You are now in the middle of this shantytown community, too far in to turn around and exit gracefully. The advantages of all that you are and have make it possible for you to walk through this community, and these same advantages are why the local people who watch you will not walk through your community back home. You have the mobility to turn back toward the city, with its modern amenities and cultural attractions. Shantytown residents, by contrast, might not be able to move through more wealthy neighborhoods without being suspected and questioned. What are you doing here? they may be asked. Are you here to steal, cause trouble, fight? We are watching you.

Vexed, you begin to worry how you come across. How does your curiosity to learn and witness and be respectful and friendly press up against history, your passport, and the pools of stagnant water? You might not be so wealthy in your home country, but here, on the streets of this urban slum, you feel like a walking bank vault, a gazillionaire in motion. Self-conscious, you hurriedly put away your expensive water bottle in the hopes that your from-somewhere-else-ness is less glaring. Your heart pounds and your insubstantial breath does nothing to oxygenate your limbs. Eyes downcast and heart bursting with grief, you push on ahead toward the Accra sea, the Dadar station, the Coronation Market: anywhere but where you are.

Guilt and the Reckoning

Our travels through different zones as someone with more advantages than local residents can wring our emotions like wet laundry. Encounters with different people may make us feel glad, sad, mad, or bad. Our travels through different zones might also elicit various

responses from the local communities with whom we interact. People who meet us might also feel glad, sad, mad, or bad. Everyone involved might exhibit a range of responses, for there is no one way for any of us to act, no foolproof formula to follow.

These two stories might resonate with you if you've traveled abroad to resource-poor countries or areas. Having more of something—wealth, global mobility, or education, for example—doesn't always translate to knowing what to do with it. We well-intentioned Western travelers, as we notice the inequality all around us, often retreat from engagement with local people for fear of coming off as insensitive or brash, for fear of not knowing how to handle all the emotions that feel raw. The promise of the frosty pint or the wish to be anywhere but here—where we are—are ways that the discomfort we feel hijacks the moment and pulls us toward a less-stressful escape.

I'm not saying that such moments like the ones these two stories depict won't make us feel discomfort. I'm sure they will, and they certainly have for me many times. An ethical and engaged life for me means grappling with the reality that I and my students have more opportunities in life than many of the people we meet on our travels abroad, as well as millions of people we will never meet both at home and far away.

While all this is true, here's what I've also learned: In the midst of a guilt trip, I focus in on my own discomforting feelings, leaving space for nothing and no one else. I turn into an echo chamber, reproducing and strengthening the disempowering feelings. Whether I share a common language with the local people or not, on multiple occasions, I've fled from interactions, wishing to be anywhere but where I was. The times where I've short circuited or fled, although supplying a short moment of relief, haven't felt as liberating as I had hoped they would. Instead, I've felt deflated and dispirited.

People I meet with fewer resources and less opportunity than I have don't need my pity (I can't think of anyone who needs my pity, for that matter). They do need my respect, understanding, and acknowledgement though—things I'm only able to offer if I am still engaged and present in the interaction. I now know that the people who I've stepped away from because of my own soupy guilt are people whose dignity, desire to be heard, and dreams for themselves and their families are just as valid and compelling as mine and yours. When I more mindfully breathe through these moments of real inequity between me and others, I do so less to pretend it's not happening or it doesn't matter and more to be present and grounded in where I am and who is around me, even though these very things make me feel awfully squirmy.

Learning how to stay present, breathe through my feelings, and recognize the dignity of the people around me is one critical strategy I've adopted to help displace the mesmerizing hold of guilt trips and my desire for easy escape. In this way, I'm practicing how to make the moment less about me and my squirmy feelings, and more about the context and the people who inhabit it when I stay present.

The Ladies, Their Lives, and Her Arm around My Waist

It's 4pm on a warm afternoon, and I'm with a group standing around two women squatting side by side on a street in a village in South India. The women's saris are folded under their knees as they busily arrange clumps of grain to dry on newspapers spread like a bedsheet on the road. I have my students with me and one of my Indian partners who is an environmental and social science researcher, Ms. Bhargavi. We've come to this village to better understand what happens to urban poor communities that rarely enjoy the glitter of globalization. Earlier in the day, Bhargavi had described for us the pressures on natural habitats, water, and trees and of pollution. We're in this community now to learn about the pressures on people.

Bhargavi explains this to the women drying grain on the road. They lift their faces at us only momentarily, barely nod, and nonchalantly resume their activity. It's like we're not even here—this gangly out-of-place group of foreigners on a semi-paved road that skirts an embankment of a lake—but of course, here we are. The drying grains on the newspapers make patterns like bird wings and elephant ears. My students and I stand in small groups watching the women work.

Bhargavi asks the women about their lives: How long have you lived here? Are you able to make ends meet? What are some challenges you face? To the Western sensibility, the questions seem blunt and invasive. The women though, delight at the unexpected press conference. They turn away from their grains and turn toward us, enthusiastically diving into a tell-all. It's like an invisible on-switch has been activated, transforming the barely nodding women a moment ago into big-gestured actors on stage. We learn many details about their life and community: three hundred people live in this village, a mediocre government school educates their children, and the hospital and medical shop are located farther away. Most women in the community work in agriculture or as domestic help in richer people's homes. Their menfolk work in the fields, or on construction sites, as drivers or petty tradesmen.

"All of us used to farm land," one woman says, "but there is less tillable land now because of all the construction." She points her chin to the bones of a high-rise apartment complex being built across the lake. "Small plot farmers like us are suffering." When Bhargavi asks why, all the women talk at once, for there is much to say. They explain how the urban building boom and attendant pressures on the out-laying land have led to increased pollution in their community and decreased access to clean water.

Another woman asks, "How long will we be able to use this water?" I'm reminded of scholar Shazia Rahman's work that brings together postcolonial feminism and the environment. She writes, "Belonging includes *both* social and environmental justice in terms of distribution of natural resources and political participation." The women's stories illustrate how everything in their lives is connected, so that what happens to the lake is what happens to their health, well-being, and ability to work.

Another woman scans our group, perhaps assessing us, maybe gathering her thoughts. "The construction debris makes our children sick. Our families are ill. Our jobs and neighbors are here, but without clean water, what will happen to us? Where will we go? Isn't this our city too? We work so hard to make ends meet with so little. We too deserve a good life, don't we?" She and the other women nod at each other and turn back to their grains.

The women's energy aston-ishes me. They deal with so much on a regular basis, and now own their story in front of a group of strangers. The details of their lives, like their monthly salary or home construction costs, help locate them economically. Telling us about the foods they eat, their caste, or family background—or even explaining in detail the raw humiliation that one woman experienced moments after she birthed her child at the nearby government clinic because of her poorness—similarly locates them socially. When the villagers throw open the details that many Westerners meticulously guard as "private," the telling and sharing actually confers worth upon their own lives. Yes, the women face innumerable barriers and must navigate a regimented social hierarchy. As we listen to their stories, though, we begin to realize that they also handle their days of struggle with agency and determination. They joke with each other and laugh together while they work side by side. They speak for us to hear, but they also speak for themselves. When the women narrate their story to us and each other, we feel dignity hold together their words and spirit.

I step back and survey the scene; everything seems to be going well. The village women share and tell, laugh and joke. My students also seem to be doing well. Even though they don't understand the real-time interactions and must wait for English translations from Bhargavi or me, they remain engaged. The slap-slap sounds of the grain hitting the newspapers on the street provide a metronome to the afternoon's rhythm. Reading about water insecurity and uneven development in a Western college classroom is one thing; standing in a circle around these women as they say, share, voice, and make known the gritty complexities of their lives is visceral. It feels embodied, insistent, urgent, and real. Here, learning comes alive.

If everything seems to be going so well, I wonder, why then do I feel so terribly wrong? I swallow my discomfort, try to focus, and rejoin the group.

Friendly Her, Checked-Out Me

A few more women from the village curiously approach us. One slides alongside me and listens as I translate. When I smile at her, she drapes her arm around my waist familiarly. I feel the heat from her skin merge with mine. Within minutes we start to chat amicably and laugh freely. At least, that's what it looks like to someone watching us. To report the scene more accurately though, only the lady next to me chats amicably and laughs freely. I, on the other hand, try to participate in the conversation but feel brittle and discombobulated. For the last few minutes as we've talked, my discomfort has reached a crescendo. The dull ache I've been feeling now pinches into a cramp. Increasingly, I'm thinking a lot about who I am, what I have, and how I might be perceived—all in relation to the lady whose arm is around me and the women of her community.

These women face challenges I've never faced before and likely never will. My healthcare, education, and access to opportunities look so different than the stories we've been hearing this afternoon. The weight of our history and present seems overwhelming. Though I navigate themes of advantage and inequality all the time—it's been the stuff of my work for decades, in fact—today I just cannot process it all. I am a soggy sponge that cannot hold even another drop. Something about today feels unnavigable, and no matter what I do, I feel off, wrong, and ashamed of things I had no control over.

And so, to protect myself from going under, I mentally escape. My attention wanders and I check out. I dim my eyes and cork my ears from the lady who chats and laughs next to me. She speaks, but I can't hear her.

I know I'm not alone in feeling this way. Has this ever happened to you? You're somewhere outside of your usual life, maybe in a South Indian lake community for the afternoon. Or a Malian women's cooperative. Or the Brazilian rainforest. Or walking through an urban slum. Maybe you're just on a different bus in your own city or volunteering in an afterschool program, and suddenly, the weight and guilt and history of having what you have, all that you have access to, all that you've never had to experience because of the advantages you've been born with feels heavy and punctures your heart. Not heavy in a burdensome and ungrateful way, but heavy in a why is the world so unjust kind of way. We soak in guilty discomfort like a bitter tea that's been steeping for too long. Such moments knock us upside the head. It's hard to know what to do with guilty feelings.

Guilt, Deconstructed

Slowing down our thoughts helps us better understand what's going on when we find ourselves in the pit of sticky, cloying guilt. Global guilt floods our senses not because we've done something explicitly wrong, but because we realize that we benefit from an unjust and unequal system. We realize that our lives are propelled by advantages and privileges that have been conferred upon us without any say in the matter. Our wrongness, if we can even call it that, manifests without our agency, and contributes to the business-as-usual model in which some people have more than most others.

One reason we feel guilt is because we desire more than is offered by the business-as-usual model of inequity. We desire a more equitable world, or at least, a world that isn't unassailably more difficult for so many of us, and by extension, easier for others of us closer to the mythic norms of our societies. There's a gap between our own ideals of fairness and equity, and the inherently inequitable system in which we live. When we feel we have somehow failed our own ideals by benefiting from the inequitable systems that make life more difficult for others, that's precisely the gap in which guilt finds a hospitable home. We have not created the systems that have given us the privileges of our birth, race, family, gender, sexuality, wealth, or citizenship status. But learning about and witnessing how our privileges play out—especially in contexts where we hear from people without such privileges—can bring us right to that uncomfortable gap between our ideals and reality.

For me, the gap feels like a hectic storm, a complex assortment of feelings that cloud and mask the sun. As a shorthand I call this emotional response "guilt," but it includes helplessness, disappointment, sadness, and anger. I experience guilt as a cacophony of feelings—sometimes the anger feels more acute, while at other times the sadness crests and takes the lead.

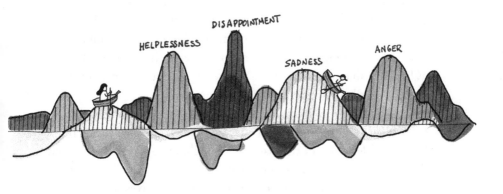

When I feel guilty, I'm trying to make sense of many interrelated issues at once: the inequality that I was born into, the broad-scale institutional systems that perpetuate inequality, the crimes of the past and present, and my own better-off position. And because guilt isn't only linked to one source or one emotion, it's a difficult feeling to unpack and redirect.

Guilt: Productive or Not?

Is guilt productive? Well, this is debatable. On the one hand, feeling the flood of emotions as we notice the equity and opportunity gaps in our world can wake us up. Our awareness of ourselves and others grows and deepens. We might then feel activated, more inspired, and determined to make change in our communities. The emotional jolt from feeling guilty, in this case, serves as the nourishing root from which courage and right action can blossom.

On the other hand, though, emotional floods and jolts can also short circuit our brains and drown our hearts. Rather than catalyze right action, guilt can grab our feet like quicksand and suck us under. It's not so long before the questions and self-recriminations begin: What does it mean that I have more than other people? Should I have what I have, enjoy what I enjoy? Do I deserve this? Perhaps I don't. What a terrible person I am . . . With each passing sentence, the guilt and shame silently fractures our attention.

When we feel guilty and shameful over something we didn't knowingly do, we might lash out to protect ourselves, sometimes becoming defensive or combative. We might altogether turn off, shut down, distract ourselves, or rationalize our pain away. What unites all these behaviors is a loud preoccupation with ourselves. I don't know about you, but when I'm thrashing around feeling guilty or shameful over something, I'm not very present to what is in front of me. I'm preoccupied and distracted, for guilt sucks up the energy and takes up a lot of space. My mind prattles, and I construct elaborate soliloquies over my own righteousness or sense of being wronged. Focused solely on myself, I become a self-obsessed island with little care left for those around me.

If we're too focused on our guilt and berating ourselves for having more than the person in front of us, how will we ever silence our minds enough to really listen to someone else's story? I'm not suggesting that in our quest to better navigate guilt we forget how inequality does play out or why the system is so unfair. But—can we simultaneously acknowledge that the differences between us sometimes matter greatly, *and* step toward one another with our full attention and presence?

Guilt, Far or Near

Though many of us feel guilt—some, like me, feel it as a physical presence—we don't really talk enough about it because it's uncomfortable and makes us feel bad. Rather than be isolated on our own, wouldn't it be more helpful if we were able to, instead, speak together about how to name and then navigate our guilt? Naming, of course, is the first step to navigating. That's why I've shared my stories throughout this book in detail as a beginning, an offering: "I felt this. This was difficult or confusing for me." And in turn, my small story invites you to consider: how about you? What do you feel as you watch the local people watch you as you walk through their community in Ghana, India or Jamaica? How does that frosty lager taste in the jungle-themed bar with other foreigners and expats laughing loudly all around you? Is it so easy to swallow down your feelings?

If we could quiet the guilty judgmental chatter in our minds and breathe with more clarity, I think we might be able to stay more present in uncomfortable moments and offer small glimpses of justice. Justice, in this case, isn't always about fixing what's broken. Sometimes, justice to me looks like us holding space for one another, to witness and hear one another's story in the grace of a loving heart. It might sound hokey or too simple or not-so-radical, but holding space for one another across different realities is really hard to do.

Back in the South Indian village, when I turned away from the lady with her arm around my waist, I chose the familiarity of nursing my guilt and shame. I didn't know how to solve any of the mammoth issues that complicated her life and the lives of the women in her community, and so I simmered in the shame of my impotence. I later realized I was actually turning away from not only her but myself as well. True presence with others is predicated upon true presence with ourselves. I wasn't in the village to fix anything or make any big promises. All I had to do was be present and appreciate the moments of sharing.

Stand Up to Guilt: Don't Recline

"Are they church people?" the lady with her arm around my waist asks me, gesturing toward my students. It's some time later, and she had left our group and now has rejoined. We've taken a tour of the village, and spoken to a few more people. I've continued to listen to the conversations and translate for my students, but I have also been somewhat wrapped up in my own mind. I am working to be present with what is in front of me, and not sink back into the familiar patterns of shame and guilt that lure me in like a comfortable sofa.

"Church people? Oh no, not at all," I reply. We speak together in the local language Kannada. She holds my gaze and waits for me to say more, so I continue. "These young people are all students, university students from America who want to understand how different kinds of people live in such a big city. The fancy malls and new construction tell one story, but you and your village community tell another. That's why we've come here to meet you and listen."

She waggles her head in that South Asian sideways way that indicates—among other things—*ah yes, I see.* "They've traveled so far simply to learn!" she says, applauding not only these students' journey but a broader educational system that encourages such far-flung sojourns. "Sometimes, the teachers at the nearby school do not even come to class because they do not receive their salaries for months on end. Tell me, if the government gives no money for teachers and no teachers come to the school to teach, how will our children learn and grow up to do big and important things? What chance will our children have to raise their own families and provide food for their young ones?"

I nod my head sympathetically. I can't even begin to compare the educational system she describes with that of my students and mine—we, who already have so much in this world, can travel so far simply to amass even more knowledge and experience. How is this possible that we can live in the same world with such different experiences? I start to lean back into the familiar guilty sofa, but then catch myself. Don't recline, I tell myself. Sit up straight. I gently inhale into the moment to keep myself present and grounded. I exhale the feeling that I have to fix everything. I'm just one person, I tell myself. I'm here only to be open to the stories my new friend offers me, and to offer her the gift of my full self. I breathe in and out attentively and meet her gaze. I am here, right here, and nowhere else.

She reaches across me and picks up a few strands of my hair. Something imperceptible seems to have shifted between us. I can't be sure, but I feel like my commitment to be present invited her to take another step forward toward me. She inspects the white hair on my head peppered in between all the black strands. "You don't dye your hair?" she asks. I shake my head and smile. "And you are the teacher for these students?" Again I nod, and this time, I am oddly shy.

"My parents are from Bangalore and Mysore," I explain, "and have been settled in America for many years. I grew up there but come to India often."

She and I stand aside from the group and talk about our families. We discover we are the same age. We both have two kids. She asks me questions. I answer. I tell her a bit about my life. She tells me about her life, and I learn a little more about what makes it difficult, what makes it ordinary, and sometimes, what makes it even wonderful. Occasionally, the guilty judgement and chatter in my mind threaten to pull me away, and each time, I consciously pause my thoughts to focus on my new friend. We talk for a long time, and toward the end of our conversation, she says, "Even though you live in America, you still look Indian." We both laugh.

Days later, the sweetness of her comment rings through my heart. I think back to the year and a half I spent in India when I was in my early twenties, and how the painful ache to definitively belong to either the United States or India hampered so many of my interactions with people. My new friend's funny comment about me looking Indian hasn't, of course, settled my lifelong unsettledness about where I belong. It has, though, presented me with a small gift of connection. I savor the time she and I spent together, and I hope I've presented her with my own small gift. Maybe also of connection. Maybe something else. Certainly of holding her stories with care.

Stay Present and Breathe

As I remember the feeling of laughing with the lady with her arm around my waist, I am immensely grateful for making the decision to be present to receive whatever the moment offered. I also know, though, that the process of navigating our guilt, advantages, and differential opportunities isn't as simple as breathing in and out suggests.

  Navigating difference and inequality is damn complicated. So is understanding the ways that systemic inequalities offer opportunities for some and none or less for others.

And yet, consider this: without the simple breath, without that reminder to stay present and not retreat into the sounds of our own chatter, we are even further from our goal of connecting across differences and making change—aren't we?

The idea that a simple breath can be a powerful tool to use during our travels might, I imagine, make some of us feel skeptical. It might feel easy to dismiss. How can something so small and pedestrian be radical enough, useful, or productive? I wonder if our predilection to disregard simple strategies might be related to our socialization into a system that values concepts like overwork, overtime, overthink, and over-fatigue. Many of us humblebrag that we're so tired and grumble about how much there is to do. Life coach Martha Beck sums up this concept beautifully in an acerbic quote: "Some people feel superior when they work around the clock. This is like proudly pouring Tabasco sauce in your eyes." Many of us are realizing that there's a beauty and value in being able to rest momentarily that is underrated, or more likely, devalued. Moments of breath are critical to resting, for noticing and listening can make our heads and hearts ache and break. As we rush from one thing to the next and find our thoughts tossed around, a deep cleansing breath encourages us to slow down our pace and locate ourselves amidst the noise in which we're surrounded. Rather than the sting of Tabasco, the breath provides us a gentle salve to root us in the moment, a mindful reminder to follow the ins and outs of air that travel through our body.

How great would it be if all our interactions across advantage, inequality, and differential opportunity melted into affectionate hair-touching and arm-around-waist moments like the one I shared in India. I'd like to be able to tell you that this story is emblematic of all my travels. Or that since that afternoon in the South Indian village, I've remained present and mindful in all that I do. I'd like to be able to say that I now know how to navigate guilt effectively, and I'm never tempted to dim my eyes and cork my ears to the difficult stories of struggle that I hear and witness. I'd like to say all this and more, but of course, it wouldn't be true. The actual truth is that I'm oftentimes present but not always so. Some of my interactions across difference have been painfully and utterly awful, while other moments have reminded me of the shared humanity of all of us. I do still feel the crush of anger-sadness-disappointment-helplessness for all that I have and have access to, but am training myself to respond with gratefulness and awareness. If I silence my own guilty mental chatter and stay present in an interaction, however brief, I think of this as its own kind of small justice.

If we don't try to connect in small ways with one another—knowing that we are all mired in various differences that sometimes matter a little and at other times greatly matter to our lived realities—then what is the point of our social justice ideals?

As Rick Ayers and William Ayers write in *Teaching the Taboo: Courage and Imagination in the Classroom:*

> If society cannot be changed under any circumstances, if there is nothing to be done, not even small and humble gestures toward something better; well, that ends the conversation. . . . But if a fairer, saner, and more just social order is both desirable and possible—that is, if some of us can join one another to imagine and build a participatory movement for justice, a public space for the enactment of democratic dreams—our field opens slightly.

Breathing and being present, then, isn't about solving everything or feeling solid all the time. Being present and mindful acknowledges that yes, we will feel squirmy and unsettled when we leave our more privileged bubbles and come face to face with our complex world. It urges us not to check out, and encourages us to stay present. Without a strong understanding of our guilt and shame, it is difficult to figure out what to do. The fact that all of us are born into a systemically unfair system is not our fault. Though we cannot dismantle all oppression, neither do we pretend that all is fine with the world or relinquish our responsibility in its repair. In the wise words of a trans mixed-race student of mine:

> It's hard for me to believe that my role as a person with certain privileges is truly to stay in my corner or to disappear entirely. For now it seems that my work is to accept and to understand my position and to move past feeling sorry about who I am. To engage with Seattle as a whole and to engage with the world outside of the United States is to understand my own anxiety without letting it bury me. If I can process my own advantages and step surely yet humbly over unfamiliar territory, I may be ready to accept the concrete responsibilities of being a world citizen I find along the way.

Connecting across our differences will never be simple. Yes, the world is dizzyingly complex, but we have tiny pockets of agency we can exercise. We can ask ourselves and each other: How will you move through this moment? How do you want to come across? What will you remember? When we slow down and take a cleansing breath, we realize that just because we notice difference does not mean we always need to successfully

traverse or fix it. Sometimes, all we can do is just acknowledge what is apparent. In the words of literary scholar Rajani Srikanth, "For it is only when we acknowledge that there are some chasms we cannot easily span, and yet continue in the effort to do so, that we achieve the true sense of understanding what it means to coexist in a world of disparate others."

Sometimes, the greatest act of justice available to us is to listen well and honor people's stories, to open ourselves up empty and be ready to receive. Let's not underestimate this possibility. How we receive stories and experiences from people different than us matters greatly. All of us want to be acknowledged for who we are, people in our own families and neighborhoods as well as people who live far away. As Parker Palmer writes in the *On Being Project*, "The human soul doesn't want to be advised or fixed or saved. It simply wants to be witnessed—to be seen, heard and companioned exactly as it is." While a simple and mindful breath might not lead to all the answers we seek, breathing and being present, though, seems to me the only way to receive what we are offered.

- -

Holding Space Together

- There's nothing wrong with a group of foreigners relaxing together and celebrating their kinship while abroad. But in the story at the beginning of the chapter with Liam, the young man studying abroad in Kenya, something else seems to be represented at the safari-themed pub Liam escapes to. What might this be? What stands out for you in this story?

- The second story is purposefully written in second-person with "you" as the protagonist. Why might I have chosen this style at this particular point in the book, given that most of the other stories are either third or first person? How did it feel to read about "you" in this way? What stands out in this story?
- My story with the village women runs the gamut with me feeling shut down simply listening to someone else's struggles to feeling immense gratitude for all that I have. What connections can you make between my experiences recounted here and your own traveling stories? When have you "run the gamut" with another person on your own travels or closer to home?
- The practice of taking regular deep cleansing breaths cannot solve inequalities, though it can prime us to be present and hear what is offered to us. How might a strategic breath or two help focus your own head and heart? What kinds of stories or experiences have you shared with or received from others across identity and difference because you stayed present and grounded in the moment?

CHAPTER 8

- - - - - - - - - - - - - - - - - -

Helmet-to-Cheek:
Go Small and Find Joy

My journey with social justice work has been a long and confusing one. As I traveled and journeyed across various boundaries both at home and abroad, the stories of people I met brought to life the broader and deeply problematic social, economic, political, and institutional structures I was learning about and learning to critique. This was how I and many of the people around me in academia and social justice movements, too, were learning about society. We learned how to quickly scan a "text"—be it a film, novel, TV show, an organization, a syllabus, a politician's speech, or someone's real life—and pronounce our verdict of what wasn't working and why. The more we learned to identify and explain the structures that made life difficult for people, the more we picked them out wherever we were.

At some point, though, I started to think that all the negativity we were getting good at identifying and explaining could easily overwhelm our hopes for what our social justice work was actually about: a better world for more of us filled with safety, opportunity, creativity, affection, and dignity. Could we say what wasn't working without falling into the perpetual shroud of negativity? What was the role of positivity—however small—in our quest for a better world? Through my growing investment in the power of the breath to keep us grounded and present, I started to wonder: How might a different kind of breath help keep our hearts light, even as we work to repair what is broken in our world?

Helmet-to-Cheek: When in Despair, Go Small

I rest heavily in an auto rickshaw, amazed that even at this early morning hour, the push of traffic clogs the Bangalore streets. The long scarf I wear loosely around my neck serves as an ineffective pollution mask. Glancing around, my gaze drifts lazily across the scope and variety of vehicles gathered at the signal. In India, cars, buses, lorries, SUVs, bullock-carts, rickshaws, scooters, motorcycles, bicycles, and walkers all jostle for space in a configuration that seems at first wildly irrational, and then, reconsidered, simply art. I inwardly groan at the delay. I'm late to meet my students. Again. As the vehicles inch forward getting nowhere, I cannot find calm. I inhale stress and despair with each breath I take.

My rhythm of stress and despair seems to fit the larger funk I am in, not just about the traffic or being late, but also about broader, global issues. The more I learn about the world, the more I learn about greed, bigotry, violence, exploitation, divisiveness, and just plain horribleness that leaves too many people without enough. So Much Bad Stuff. Lack of resources. Corruption. Poverty. Power over others. Squashing of dignity. The greed, the want, the lack. Sitting in the auto rickshaw, my brain sags and I can't help but fret. How do I and so many of us hold all these issues—and the millions of people whose everyday lives are compromised on account of injustices—in our minds and hearts without fretting or short circuiting all the time? Once we do understand the business-as-usual model and what that means for too many people around the world, how could we not growl and rage at what is happening all around us all the time?

To slow my brain down, I urge myself to focus only on what is in front of me. Go small, I tell myself, and so I gaze at my driver's head. I notice his cool haircut, unusually cut at various lengths, and am instantly mesmerized. The closely cut spikey parts remind me of daybreak, and the long strands, like luscious nightfall. Is this fellow seriously fashion-forward, or did his barber get distracted during his

last haircut? I imagine my driver preening in front of a mirror. I imagine him styling his hair and giving himself a wink of self-affirmation every morning before setting out for the day. I smile to myself; the strategy to focus on small things right in front of me settles me a bit. I'm certainly not at peace, but am less broken about the traffic, less bothered by being late and all the horribleness of the world I cannot change.

From my driver's hair, I look to the side and see a family perched on a scooter. Go small, I tell myself again, breathe in the details. I see that the family also waits at the traffic signal like us. A man drives, and a lady who I imagine to be his wife sits behind him hugging his waist. Their five- or six-year-old child balances in front of the father's thighs while standing on the floor of the vehicle. He's in a school uniform and squirms a bit, squished up against the handle bars, but he holds on tightly. The family looks like any ordinary middle-class Indian family on a scooter on their way to school and office, one of hundreds if not thousands I will pass before reaching my destination. The family chats and laughs with each other at the traffic light. Surreptitiously, I watch, surprised at how intensely I am staring at them. My rickshaw driver with the fly hair has noticed me staring at the family. It's hard not to notice me, for I am almost hanging out of the auto. He peeks intermittently at the scooter family, and then curiously back at me via his rear-view mirror to figure out what exactly has captured my attention so.

The man on the scooter repositions his leg to balance the vehicle. The woman scoots her bottom more securely behind him and rewraps her arms around his waist. He leans back toward the woman in an affectionate gesture and brings his head toward hers. The helmet he wears is bulbous and awkward, but he nuzzles her cheek with it. She closes her eyes, a deep smile on her open dark brown face. His cool plastic helmet to her warm human cheek, they embrace in a non-embrace, a helmet-to-cheek gesture. The couple remain in repose and ease. The child feels the scooter totter and arches his body to turn around. He notes his parents: eyes closed, plastic to skin and loving one another. The boy turns back toward the front, assured that all is well. He stands at attention at the helm of the scooter. The red signal light continues to glow, stretched across the street like an invisible net holding in the assorted hoofs, wheels, tires, and feet. The couple continue to love one another a moment or two. The woman then opens her eyes and pats her partner's shoulder. He faces forward, readying the vehicle for the signal change. The woman rests comfortably behind him, arms lightly wrapped around his waist for balance. The man tousles the hair of the boy, who immediately brings his hand to his head to smoothen the ruffled strands.

Ordinary, Yet Extra Special

I take a deep breath and lean back into the padded rickshaw bench, cleansed, as if I have emerged from a hot bath. The family's affection and the couple's helmet-to-cheek love revitalizes my mood and restores my energy. I am open, scrubbed of rage and hopelessness, for the helmet-to-cheek image is the purest expression of joy I've witnessed in a long time. Such a small gesture feels at once ordinary and too easily miss-able, extraordinary and don't-look-away special. Could it be that I now understand another thin layer of life's mysterious ways?

The driver and I catch glances in the mirror. Where before I lay slumped against the sides of his vehicle in frustration, now I am made anew, anointed by the beautiful family and what they have taught me. I boldly flash my driver a big grin. His caterpillar eyebrows jump up in surprise as if they're bouncing on a trampoline. He gasps and exclaims "*Ayyo!*" a Kannada expression that can mean "Oh wow!" or "Oh no!" depending on the context. He glances away awkwardly for a moment and busies himself with the vehicle's ignition as it sputters to life. He finds me through his mirror again—our  portal of communication—and then waggles his head side-to-side in that most ubiquitous of Indian gestures. "Might as well join her," his head shake suggests. He too lets loose a brilliant smile of his own filled with night and stars and smallness and bigness. He revs the engine, and I clap my hands with glee as we zoom onward, for now the signal is green.

Later that day I share the scene with my students. I narrate the dust that crept inside my nostrils, the honking hullabaloo. I explain how injustices seemed to have won wherever I turned: in the old historic buildings torn down without remorse, the tired hawkers with less road space to sell their wares, and the potholes the size of elephants. And then I describe helmet-to-cheek, the cute kid's patience as his parents loved one another, the bouncy eyebrows and effervescent smile of my driver. I tell them what a surprisingly refreshing jolt of reality it was to remember that alongside the ever-present challenges in the world, innumerable small joys can also reveal themselves if we take a moment to be open, breathe deeply, and step toward our world with a slow and patient approach. "This feeling might stay with me all day," I say. I am equal parts earnest and corny.

Yes, Social Justice Work Can Include Joy

I did not know it at the time, but the scooter scene did indeed stay with me, and for much longer than a day. Surprisingly, the story also attached itself to many of the students as well. Something about helmet-to-cheek transcended its particular moment and directly spoke to us. Perhaps it was the odd plastic-to-skin imagery, or my enthusiastically earnest and corny retelling. Maybe the scene slowed down time through an everyday appreciation of what was in front of us. Or maybe we all just needed permission to focus on joy a tiny bit more than we usually did without feeling like social justice sellouts.

Many of us in my group had felt fatigued by the incessant examples of injustice we saw both at home in the United States and now in India. We believed in social justice, and hence, spent our time identifying injustices. In fact, "being a good critical thinker" meant we continually rehearsed how unjust configurations of power and privilege were playing out everywhere and always.

And they do and are—don't get me wrong. But trafficking in only one set of ideas simultaneously highlights and diminishes what is in front of us. Once we form a view, we embrace information that confirms that view while ignoring and sometimes even rejecting information that casts doubts on it. As Chris Yates and Pooja Sachdev write in their book *Rewire: A Radical Approach to Tackling Diversity and Difference*, "Even when we think we are objectively seeking evidence, studies have found that we are more likely to seek out, favor, and remember information that confirms the beliefs we already hold (and we are more likely to forget or fail to notice information that goes against our assumptions)." This phenomenon is called confirmation bias, and most of us are quite good at it. We pick and choose which pieces of information to include in our purview so as to confirm our views and preexisting beliefs. So when we look for injustices, that's exactly what will be highlighted. And while we absolutely do need to focus on how people and institutions reproduce power unfairly, does our exclusive focus on these views diminish or dampen what else we see, notice, hear, and witness around us? I am starting to think so. Like many social justice advocates, my students and I had become so good at noticing the wrongs that we had become less skilled at recognizing and being present for the rights, no matter how small they were.

Here, though, was a moment of pure joy, a joy that was so noteworthy in its ordinariness we felt special simply contemplating it. No wonder helmet-to-cheek struck a chord with us. Throughout our time in India that summer, my students and I spoke often about helmet-to-cheek as a shorthand for the unexpected joy we might recognize if we simultaneously expanded what we looked for and breathed in these moments with intentionality and presence. We collectively called these small-yet-big moments helmet-to-cheeks, and we shared them with each other throughout our time abroad.

One student conveyed this story in a paper he wrote:

I sat by myself at a roadside stall for a cup of chai. Two or three other people sat on low plastic stools eating a snack or drinking their tea. I was the only white guy in the small restaurant, and a man who looked like he was the owner nodded at me in greeting. A young boy sat across from me on a bench, and I found myself becoming irritated, defensive, and suspicious. Is this kid going to ask me for money or something? Will I be able to enjoy my chai in peace? Here in India as a foreigner, I'm often the recipient of outstretched hands and way too much attention, and it was starting to wear on me. I arranged my face in a scowl, hoping to dissuade the boy from approaching me. The owner then walked purposefully to the boy and bent down. The man and boy touched foreheads in an odd but intimate gesture of love. They both closed their eyes and breathed in each other's warmth. The man then stood up, approached me and asked me, "What will you have, sir?" His hand rested comfortably on his son's shoulder. Both father and son smiled at me, and I felt like an ass for my rude demeanor. But then I breathed in the warmth of the moment myself and enjoyed their love. It was my own helmet-to-cheek moment.

Months after we returned home from our study abroad program, another student sent me this note:

Our program has been reverberating within me the last couple of days. . . . I've been feeling really crushed by this cruel world. I cried yesterday watching 'Law and Order.' I cried reading an article about a reality TV star's miscarriage. I cried just now reading about the recent shooting. It all seems like too much, the big things as well as the dumb little things. So I'm sitting here, overwhelmed by a world I've shut out for finals. I'm trying to write a paper on physical vapor deposition but can't stop thinking that this world is damn cruel, so, so cruel. And then, I thought of our words "helmet-to-cheek, helmet-to-cheek," and remembered that joy and love also exist. Just wanted to let you know that our words are still hugging my soul even after so many months!

Find the Joy: A Critical *and* Compassionate Lens

A social justice lens enables us to recognize, name, and combat oppressions. So many people both in our local communities and farther away suffer needlessly, and a commitment to social justice means we notice, witness, and pay attention to people's struggles and lives unlike ours. It's important to remember that injustice is cross-cultural and cross-geographical in its reach: there's nothing particularly "Global South-y" about injustices, for injustices flourish everywhere that people are. Be it Des Moines or London or Perth, one need not journey to far-off Dhaka or Lingongwe or Pretoria to feel fatigued or overwhelmed by the failures of quality opportunities for all. In our own home contexts, the scale of injustice might *look different* than it might in other contexts, yet life is neither easy nor equitable for all.

Helmet-to-cheek moments recognize something bigger than ourselves—a lifeline toward goodness, a way to "find the joy" even when it seems in our complicated and unjust world there is little to spare. Such moments indicate a loving force extraordinarily special, yet so ordinarily obvious. In our quest to root out inequality and our desire to repair the ills of the world, sometimes the obvious small moment of something else is easy to miss. If we train our gaze solely on unfairness and injustice, how will we then catch glimmers of goodness and wonder? A funky haircut, a beautiful smile, someone resting their body against another balanced on a scooter, the curve of a father's arm around his son's shoulders—all everyday scenes that we have seen hundreds of times. Sometimes, though, the everyday moments we stumble upon grow in scope, and present themselves from a different angle precisely when we are ready to bear witness and see differently.

When we are reminded that everyday joyfulness exists—even in the midst of grim challenges—the image prompts us to look up from our agitated state and focus our gaze more softly. This joy in the midst of challenges differentiates helmet-to-cheek from more conventional encouragements to "stop and smell the roses" and "enjoy the simple pleasures of life." Rather than a straight up shot of sugar, by helmet-to-cheek I mean a kind of critical *and* compassionate lens that searches for goodness as it also notes and works toward what needs to be repaired. I'm not pretending that things aren't that bad for too many people (because they are), or that injustices are somehow easy to remedy (because they aren't). If we believe that more of us should be able to lead lives with less strife and more justice and opportunity, we have a lot of work to do on the many injustices that animate our lives. But, what if we do breathe deeply now and then and prepare to receive the joy, beauty, and love that *also* animate our lives? Might we feel something small shift in our outlook? If we individually and collectively feel a bit less worn out and burdened and, at least momentarily, a bit more hopeful and heartened with possibility, what might be possible?

Holding Space Together

- What might be seductive in the habitual practice of looking for what's not working well for everyone?
- What are ways you can "go small" in your life, especially in times of discomfort and stress?
- Holding compassion *and* criticality in our understanding of the world (or ourselves, even) can be challenging, given our mainstream "this or that" framework. Consider what an "and" approach might help us see or understand differently than the usual "or" choice. If we do open ourselves to receive what is in front of us, how might the "and" approach help us more authentically hold the various emotions we experience whether we're speaking about social justice as a broad concept or, on a smaller scale, our own sense of belonging within our families and communities?
- What kinds of helmet-to-cheek moments have you experienced either on your travels abroad or closer to home? What do you think made these moments pedestrian yet special, everyday yet astonishing? If you were to give a name to what you experienced, what would it be?
- In her essay "Change the Culture, Change the World," transnational artist Favianna Rodriguez helps us understand how social justice work requires a variety of different modes and methods. Traditional activism often includes political campaigns, protest movements, and grassroots organizers. This has been thought of as the "action spaces" of social justice. Rodriguez shares with us how the "idea spaces" of social justice are just as important, and include art, culture, and the complex heart spaces of peoples' sentiments and emotions.

Consider these two modes of social justice work. Which realm are you most comfortable in and why? What are the ways we might valorize and denigrate either action space or idea space at different moments in our desire for change and justice? How might seeking joy in a helmet-to-cheek way contribute to both the action and idea spaces of our work and movements?

- -

CHAPTER 9

- - - - - - - - - - - - - - - -

Goings and Comings in an Unequal World:

The Journey Continues

COMING HOME DOESN'T ALWAYS END THE ROILING UNSETTLEDNESS WE feel during our travels. Whether we've been navigating aspects of our identity or feeling soupy guilt, our minds and hearts keep us on edge. And when we return, we often find ourselves with questions, feelings, and frustrations not yet addressed or answered. As Talya Zemach-Bersin, a scholar of American imperialism, reflects about her own study abroad program, "My semester abroad taught me that there is a vast discrepancy between the rhetoric of international education and the reality of what many students like myself experience while abroad. Although the world may be increasingly interconnected, global systems of inequality, power, privilege, and difference are always present. That is the reality that many students face during their semesters abroad and continue to think about upon their return."

In this coming-home process, how do we better hold space for ourselves and one another? How do we position ourselves to understand the shiny rhetoric of "make the most" out of our journeys abroad and its often more confounding intersections with our lives at home?

Coming Home is a "Thing"

Within the standard story of travel, we focus more on the lead-up anticipation of going somewhere and the time spent away. These are the exciting and share-worthy aspects of a trip. But what about the return back home? Many study abroad programs, volunteer experiences, and other group travels focus exclusively on the trip itself. It's a natural focus indeed, but one that leaves little energy for either pre-trip intellectual preparation or post-trip processing. And while yes, we should be excited about and focused on our goings, many of our trips abroad are left in mid-air without sufficient and thoughtful take-offs and landings. Unpacking our mind and hearts of the experience of being elsewhere—we know—can take weeks, months, years, or even a lifetime. Coming home is often imagined as the final chapter of the traveler's tale, where our hero (or zero) begrudgingly settles back into their regular life. We imagine the act of coming home provides a neat resolution to all that has occurred, the denouement of a captivating adventure. Conflicts resolved, plot lines squared away: The End.

It's totally understandable why we downplay the coming home aspect of travel. Rarely do we understand traveling as part of a longer and holistic process. Rarely also do we create time or space to emotionally process our travels. We say, "Going abroad is hard. Coming home should be easy," but our experiences might not follow such logic.

I give a talk at a "now that you're back home from your travels" conference. Many students share their stories with me, such as this one: "Coming back home honestly seemed more unpredictable and stressful than getting used to my few months in Cambodia," a twenty-year-old woman from Michigan explains. "I expected to struggle there, but didn't expect that I'd struggle when I came home. This was my home, a place I supposedly knew how to do everything. I knew the language, the culture, and how to wash clothes! Why then was it so hard for me?"

Here's another student who spent three months in Malawi: "Culture shock hits you hard when you land in Africa, and it's for your own good. But when you come back home, everyone assumes that you're back in your familiar environment. Everyone assumes you're okay, but that wasn't the case for me at all. Returning back home to Houston felt like a more acute version of culture shock than when I arrived in Malawi. But it felt stupid to say that out loud."

Short and Surface: How Conversations Usually Proceed

If you've gone anywhere remotely considered exotic, prepare for the question, "How was your trip?" that will be asked as soon as your plane back home touches the tarmac. This ubiquitous prompt acknowledges your recent whereabouts and demonstrates polite interest. It is the infamous opening line, the one we have come to expect from everyone.

Though "how was your trip?" is a common question, it doesn't mean we always know how to answer it. Any number of these responses might rattle around for airtime:

> What do I say about my trip?
> How do I say it?
> Aaahhh!
> I'm actually not sure how my trip was.
> How can I explain my month or semester or year to somone in 5 minutes?
> Will they get what I'm saying?
> Do they actually care?
> Do I give the one-page answer or the thirty second version?
> How do I convey the gut-wrenching and soul-stirring moments in a sound bite?
> If I start to explain "how it really was," will they have the patience to hear me out?

And because the cacophony of responses tumbles around our brain like clothes in a dryer, we might retreat into safety with any number of short replies:

"It was great!"
"Amazing!"
"Awesome!"
"It was hard."
"Super-interesting!"

Our short and pat responses save us—as well as our asker—from the awkwardness of real conversation. Polite chitchat conventions maintained, everyone goes about their business (as usual).

Sometimes, though, the bold and more honest sentiments about our time abroad peek out. They bubble forth and volcano outwards. We might want to actually share some of what we experienced. Maybe we'd like to confess what was difficult. Brag about how we adapted better than we had originally thought. Or state that indeed, we've come home changed. People ask, "So, how was it?" and we squeal to ourselves, "Ooh! Maybe I'll say what I really want to say!" and so we say:

"It totally changed my life! I have so much to tell you!"
"I've never experienced anything like it! Being away encouraged me to confront things I didn't even know were in me!"
"I can't even begin to convey what it was like!"

Once in a while, you may hear these musical dreamy words:

"Really? That's awesome! Quick, let's have a cup of tea together *right now* so you can tell me all about it! I'm so intrigued, and want to hear more!"

Most often though, you'll hear,

"Really? That's awesome! Okay then. See ya around, catch ya later."

Here you are with all this volcanic-ness bursting forth with nowhere for your lava to flow. Where are the real conversations that go beyond the surface? Perhaps you want to share how you felt in the middle of your moving conversation with the Senegalese fisherwoman or the chorizo seller in Mexico. Maybe you want to talk about what it felt like to be on display all the time, or what it meant for you to see homes made of mud or tin for the first time. These are important conversations that help us figure out our thoughts, and by extension, our ethics around travel, identity, human rights, and justice. When friends and family enthusiastically like your photos on social media but fail to show up in more meaningful ways, you might feel discombobulated, disjointed, or dejected. Even a tad bit lonely.

If you recently returned from an intense trip and you feel like an active volcano, low-stakes polite chitchat might not feel all that satisfying. We might feel misunderstood and disappointed that "no one cares or understands what I'm going through" or "no one has taken the time to hear about my travels." And while the disappointment may well be rooted in the people around us who may not have time or interest to help you process your travels, this isn't just their failing. Something larger and institutional is also in operation, steering us away from focused and sustained engagement in favor of something quick and on the surface. Our modern lives are not set up for deep, thoughtful, and meaningful exchanges around hard-to-articulate ideas about identity, travel, and difference. Talk like that—as well as the conversations we're having throughout this book—requires genuine care and time. When we encourage one another to process our journeys in community, we interrupt business-as-usual thinking and living to offer each other alternatives.

More focused conversation on our travels can help us mindfully breathe and move through both those squirmy moments in the field as well as how we make sense of them when we return home. Deep breathing, in this case, reminds us to go slow and that our journeys are as of yet still unfinished. When we don't sift through, sort out, process, and piece together our experiences from abroad, it's difficult to feel settled now that we're home about all the unsettledness we experienced. Unsettledness that never settles rarely disappears; it just manifests in other ways. Let's be brave and talk together about our travels abroad and our process of coming home to expand the conversation about globalization and how our world is connected or not. Slowing the conversation down—to be present and to be brave and sit with what feelings come up—helps us better understand how our goings there affect our comings here.

Connections between the Goings and Comings

Before your journey abroad, you might have taken for granted the privileges and opportunities resplendent in your own life. You thought going abroad, you're just a regular and average person in the world. Coming home, maybe you think you are a very different kind of regular and average person than most people in the world. Your Global South goings shine light on larger structural forces of history and opportunity. Perhaps abroad you've seen more stark inequality than you've seen at home, and now you're sensitized and open. Perhaps you've seen people live with a fraction of the things you routinely discard. The more sanitized and comfortable Global North context to which you return seems now oddly overly sanitized and overly comfortable. Now that you are home, you're sure you could never go back to living the wasteful life you once did. You're beginning to grasp the material consequences of difference. Is inequality of this type unfair?

Of course. Will you have feelings about it? Of course, how could you not? Will you always know how to address all that you've seen abroad, and now, are more open to seeing similar circumstances closer to home? Certainly not. You will, though, stretch, go slow, and keep trying.

Here are two Western travelers reflecting on their time abroad, one in Pakistan and the other in Mozambique. The first is a colleague of mine, and the other, a student.

> When I visited my family in Pakistan last year, the whole area I was in had power only twelve hours a day. The electricity would be on for an hour, then off for an hour. On again, off again. When I returned home to Seattle, I couldn't flip on the lights in my living room without thinking that my sister in Pakistan couldn't do the same. It took me a long time to not feel overwhelmed with all that I had taken for granted in my regular life.

> I lived pretty simply during my time in Mozambique, better than many locals, for sure, but not crazy-extravagant. When I got home, things that I once thought were normal freaked me out, like the grocery stores overflowing with stuff and choices. All that stuff and choice paralyzed me. I just couldn't deal. How could I ever get used to this over-consumptive lifestyle again? I resisted vehemently at

first, but the sad part is that I sort-of *did* get used to it. I'm holding on to that *sort-of* because that's the part that acknowledges I was somewhere else and knew other ways of living.

Treating the coming-home process as a "thing" gives the well-intentioned traveler the permission, time, and space to figure out how we feel about our travels and what that means for the world in which we live. Coming home unsettles us, kind of like jetlag, but bigger, kind of like deja vu, but different. If we acknowledge that, yes, the trip is over but our messy feelings around the journey have yet to be resolved, I think we'd be better able to connect our global experiences and our local lives at home. Maybe then we'd be more able to see how all politics are local, even when we are addressing the global.

As writer and activist William Rivers Pitt instructs in his article, "Tip Your Server and Save the World,"

> Tip your server, don't be a jackass about it, and worry about the rest of the world after you do what is right within reach of your arm. Maybe, if you're really interested in helping your community, work towards establishing higher wages for the people who bring you food when you go out to eat; there are thousands of them right where you live. First things first; if you shaft the person making slave wages who feeds you and then go home to whine on Facebook about the poor, poor people from somewhere else, you're as much a part of the problem as the people in Washington dropping bombs and deploying drones. All politics is local.

We need not necessarily have to travel to think about equity and making a difference. But if we are given the privileges to experience other societies and meet new people, then what good is learning from your global travels if you're not going to put it to use when you get home?

Holding Space Together

- Which issues did you learn about abroad that ignited your curiosity or flamed your passions? How do those issues connect with local issues closer to home? What is the "local version" of the international issue?
- How close to or far away from that mythic norm are the people in your local community whose stories you haven't had to engage with? How have you been educated to highlight certain perspectives and perhaps erase others?
- What do we do with what we have learned abroad? Who will listen, how will they listen, and how will we tell? What about what we experienced, witnessed, heard, felt, smelled, thought, and saw during our travels abroad are to share out loud with others? What are avenues and mediums to do so? What, though, are meant for us to reflect upon and nurture on our own?
- It's not helpful to drown in guilt every time we turn on our light switch at home, thinking about people who don't have access to electricity so freely or routinely elsewhere. And yet, the connection my colleague made with her sister's experience in Pakistan moved her greatly. How do we make sense of the different experiences in this case? What would you suggest to

this traveler or, say, the traveler who becomes quickly over-whelmed at the taken-for-granted excesses in the Western gro-cery store?

- What is meant by "all politics is local"? Let's consider: Is "not being an ass" enough of a stance? What would it look like to, yes, be a better human *and* begin to interrupt the business-as-usual power structures that uphold inequity and oppression?

Expand the Conversation—Act and Do Differently

I meet a young woman named Vasanthi at a local South Asian com-munity event. When she finds out that I work on issues of identity and travel, she begins to share her thoughts about the study abroad program in Berlin, Germany, from which she recently returned:

> I'm struck at the insularity of some of my white classmates. When I was in Germany recently, my classmates continu-ally expressed amazement when we learned about the dis-crimination some Arab, Muslim, and South Asian immi-grants have faced, and the status of migrant populations. I mean, it *is* shocking because nobody should be treated that way. But in a way, I'm also not so shocked. Are they really that shocked that some white Germans are hostile to Arab, Muslim, and South Asian immigrants? The details are different in Germany, but similar things are happening in the US. Don't my classmates know how race, migration, and economics play out in the US and what some people have to face and endure? How is it that they are so naive about what happens in their own country and their own

community? I feel like I'm always the person in class that has to say something about race or some topic like that, otherwise, nothing gets said.

An African American student named Shay and I meet each other in a large and bright cafeteria. We've come to the University of California Berkeley for a national writing workshop. She's sitting with someone who's a friend of mine, and we get to talking about study abroad issues. Shay tells me she had helped organize an event at her university, a small liberal arts college in Georgia. Sponsored by the Black Student Union and the International Education office, the first-of-its-kind workshop created a space for students to reflect on the politics of race and study abroad. While the workshop was advertised to the entire campus, only African American students attended. These students felt the workshop to be a "safe space" and discussed issues of racism and white privilege, especially as they felt these ideas playing out abroad on their programs. "It was a good conversation," Shay says, appreciating the opportunity to discuss race and study abroad, "two ideas we rarely discuss together." Her voice shifts, and a lament weaves her words together. "But if only African American students are talking about race and study abroad, what are all the white students talking about? Why aren't they organizing workshops on how their own race and whiteness is connected to study abroad? Almost everybody at our university is white in terms of students, faculty, and staff. Why aren't the staff and faculty organizing workshops for white students around identity, race, and study abroad?"

When you're back home after a meaningful, jarring, or even life-changing trip, you can continue to animate your more local life with your travels abroad in a few ways. Rethink who's already talking about certain issues and expand the conversation. Who usually brings up issues of race, power, and structural advantage in your classes or wider campus community? When events focused on these topics are planned, who attends? Showing up isn't just about registering our physical presence at an event or two. It's about reframing and revitalizing the story of who we are, which issues we care about, and how we move forward with all that we have experienced.

The two examples I open this section with give us a way to reflect on the kinds of business-as-usual activities, events, and conversations that take place, where "certain" people bring up topics in class, and "certain" people convene conversations about identity, race, and study abroad. Coming home from a journey that has touched us in important ways can help shake us from this status quo in even small ways. Why not bring up topics you might not have before, or attend an event that you might not have previously? Sure, it might feel unfamiliar and a bit scary, but that's the point—right? To notice feelings, slow down thoughts, and create new patterns of communication across and amidst differences.

In the "Holding Space Together" section in chapter 8, I alluded to Favianna Rodriguez's concepts of an "idea space" and an "action space" in the work of social justice. For example, sitting with our discomfort and holding a space for each other's complexity seems to fit into the work of the "idea space" of social justice. But modifying how we "normally" think of things contributes to the "action space" as well. Anytime we're interrupting the business-as-usual model we're acting—even if it looks to be a small act. Holistic learning, like the one this book engages with, is often an iterative and generative process: new stimuli create new awareness, new awareness encourages new and different ways of being, and new ways of being result in new and different actions. It takes all parts of this learning process to transform our families and communities into more just spaces.

Acting differently can take many forms, from contributing to a discussion that might have felt "not for me" before our travels, all the way to rethinking how our travels abroad affect our everyday lives at home. Acting differently can also change how we organize our next trip, setting it on a more robust ethical foundation. The questions we ask about our programs, its pedagogy, and partnerships can illuminate business-as-usual power structures. For example, Willy Oppenheim, founder of Omprakash—an organization devoted to changing the dominant paradigm of interning and volunteering abroad to make it more ethical, affordable, and educational—asks us to consider why volunteers expect to be "placed" in host organizations abroad for a hefty fee as opposed to the more routine system of applying for and interviewing for a "position" at home. The prevailing placement model, he argues, keeps both the volunteer and the host organization unnecessarily passive while giving undue power and agency to the organizations in the middle that profit from a business model that might often be in contradiction to the "ethical partnerships" they claim to espouse. By understanding the dynamics of the business incentives and status quo formulas of voluntourism, our awareness of how our good intentions might be easily manipulated and profited upon grows. When we know better, we can choose to act better, to make different decisions the next time we travel abroad with the desire to learn about and help others.

Global health anthropologist David Citrin offers another way to act differently by providing a list of recommendations for short-term medical volunteers and programs. His list includes questions to ask and areas to research as we consider a medical mission, including this comprehensive prompt, "Critically evaluate the potential impacts of the work, both positive and negative – for yourself, the national and local health care systems, ideas about health and medical care, and the dynamics of recipient communities. This means not creating or perpetuating inequities." For programs and participating organizations, his list combines familiarity with the on-the-ground realities of low-resource settings as well as the wider dynamics of colonialism, uneven global development, and the imperial politics of Western help and aid. Two of my favorite suggestions are, "Make every effort possible to collaborate with other medical volunteer programs working nearby, and always defer to local health care institutions," and "Prepare plans with input from local institutions and communities for evaluating volunteer program impacts to ensure the work does not duplicate, disrupt, burden, or fragment existing local health care delivery." Citrin's prompts change the business-as-usual script because many Western short-term medical programs work independently of local health care facilities and do not much worry about upsetting local systems that are already present. These dynamics only foster relationships of exploitation and a one-sided so-called "global partnership" that explicitly favors the Western foreigners while implicitly devaluing the local systems.

When we better understand how our many opportunities to "travel while making a difference" might actually operate within predatory business models and profit-over-people incentives, we need to pause our enthusiasm long enough to thoroughly research the situation we're entering. Similarly, when we're abroad, stating that, "What we're doing here is okay because it's better than nothing," as a way to register our discomfort does not justify our actions if the partnerships we've entered into are unjust, prematurely celebratory, or potentially dangerous for the community in need. If we're the ones with more structural and global power, it's our responsibility to ask critical questions and research the backstory that better situates the journey, the promises made, and the local people involved. The questions we ask and research, of course, will not ameliorate everything that needs fixing, but they can help us take more responsibility regarding our choice of program, how much and to whom we are giving our money, and what our participation means to the local people. We can then take more intentional action that helps more than harms, and works to dismantle unjust structures of power.

Learning how to create social and business pathways that deviate from the status quo is a challenging process, a process that can take some time and would be better served with a good amount of patience, humor and lightheartedness. As Anne Lamott reminds us, "The road to enlightenment is long and difficult, and you should try not to forget snacks and magazines."

Holding Space Together

- So many of us who travel from the West to the Global South learn from the visceral shock of witnessing lives unlike the ones we live at home. Let's consider: What are the ethics of less-privileged communities educating those of us with more advantage and social mobility?

  Is it the far-off or closer-to-home community's responsibility to educate those of us with little exposure to different economic realities and life opportunities? What kind of burden or role does that place the community in? Should an under-resourced or minority community continue to welcome batches of advantaged students in order to help the students learn about racism, poverty, migration, or any number of issues the community members face? What's in it for the community members who are already struggling with the very issues they are to teach the students about?

- What would a meaningful exchange, a *meaningful, mutually beneficial exchange for all parties,* look like? Is that even possible, given the differences in opportunities, wealth, and privilege that different people navigate?

- Think about how you would narrate a particularly significant moment, maybe a difficult-to-be-present moment that you can now unpack and process better, or perhaps a helmet-to-cheek moment in which the ordinary seemed miraculous. How would you speak aloud each of these different travel stories and what they helped you notice, uncover, get real with, and appreciate?

• How might you metaphorically "keep in touch" with someone you've met abroad but will never see or hear from again? What does witnessing a slice of their life or hearing a part of their story mean to you now that you are back home in Akron or Calgary? What does it mean to do right by them?

- -

Global Citizenship Abroad ≠ Global Citizenship at Home?

I meet Mandy at a workshop I've offered at an arts college in Boston. She's a young white woman who's in her fourth year of college. She seems exuberant and friendly, and has just returned from a study abroad program in Cape Town, South Africa. After hearing me talk about race and study abroad, she asks if we could sit down together. "I felt bolder and more confident when studying abroad than I usually feel at home," she says, a reflective tone to her words. "I thought I should 'make the most' of my study abroad experience, and that mantra pushed me out of my comfort zone." She continues, "Something about being far from home made me feel different. As a white person and a foreigner in South Africa, it felt easier to talk to the Black students at the University of Cape Town than I usually feel talking to the few Black students on my home campus in the US," Her voice shrinks and hides and twists as she says the next part: "I'm not sure I should be saying this, but I was more comfortable with the South African Black students than I am with African Americans at home. That's okay, isn't it?"

Mandy isn't alone in sensing that it seems easier to interact with somebody who is racially and culturally different than her when she is elsewhere and far away, than it is to recognize and deal with racial and cultural differences closer to home. I've heard and observed some version of this from many young travelers. Though she's proud of putting herself out there in Cape Town, Mandy's also not the first to feel guilty and uncomfortable recognizing her monochromatic and more culturally homogenous life at home. This is the same thing we saw, in chapter 2, fueling the private college student Katherine's guilt when presenting to the high school class not far from her home campus. I'm curious, though, why many well-intentioned, advantaged students feel empowered as cultural ambassadors in one far-away context, but culturally insular and fearful in another closer-to-home context.

I've seen this dynamic over and over again. Although I am thrilled that many young adults from the West are indeed gravitating toward new experiences abroad, I cannot help but wonder what that means for the lives we lead at home. One possible reason we feel differently at home and abroad is that our relationship to economic and racial inequality can seem and feel different in the different contexts. If I travel abroad to somewhere with less wealth than my home country, as an outsider I might be able to distance myself from my own complicity in the poverty there. At home, though, it is harder to do that as I go about my day in Boston or Baddeck or Burleigh, say.

This dynamic can be rehearsed in terms of race as well. White Westerners can see themselves as more directly in conflict or competition with Black people and other people of color in the West than with, say, Black Africans in Nairobi or Sri Lankans in Colombo. The history, too, of these different places matters immensely. White Westerners might fear being confronted with their own role in the domestic situation in a way they wouldn't be abroad, so engaging with Black people and other people of color abroad might feel safer. There's also something about being a foreigner and outsider that can feel liberating and new. Travelers are often able to ask questions and make use of their unfamiliarity with the nuances of new cultures and people by becoming close to local people who serve as formal or informal guides, lovers, colleagues, and friends. Many white people traveling through the Global South, as we've seen, might also be viewed as something special, more powerful, or intrinsically worth more because of associations with class mobility, wealth, and beauty. All these dynamics play out whether we're consciously aware of them or not, and cannot but influence how Mandy and others might feel more empowered to cross difference abroad than at home. These dynamics abroad also might influence how comfortable we feel making friendships across categories of difference that could feel more entrenched at home.

Travel promises fresh starts. It makes us feel bold and untethered to the daily scripts we rehearse at home. And so, as a temporary foreigner with a finite amount of time, Mandy mobilizes her courage and commitment to make friends across racial lines while abroad. Ostensibly, this is exactly why travel can be transformative as it stretches us from the familiar and plunks us into the kinds of differences we want travelers to experience. It's a story that celebrates global citizenship, the kind of cross-cultural story that we like to highlight in newsletters, with the kind of photo that gets lots of likes on social media.

I'm not blaming Mandy or other young people who might feel more empowered abroad to cross social boundaries than they would at home. Instead, I'm emphasizing this story because it says something about the rigid intractability of social relations at home, and our expectations to be able to do something different abroad. In many cases, our programs abroad, the ones that encourage participants to "leave your comfort zone" and "engage in a multicultural world," inadvertently reinforce the binary between home and abroad, where home is where we remain regular and comfortable (and most often, racially, culturally, and economically segregated), and abroad the place where we loosen our preconceptions, capitalize on our foreigner status, and shake things up. Since so many of our conversations on identity and differences at home are mired in confusion, guilt, and shame, what would it mean to gradually build up to the big shiny goals of global citizenship? What's the connection between global citizenship success abroad and global citizenship failure at home? Interacting with people across difference while we are abroad, however well-intentioned we might be, does not make any of us a global citizen unless we are willing to rethink who we interact with at home and how. Our trips abroad need to intersect with our local lives. Otherwise, we're just exoticizing difference abroad while refusing to engage with it at home.

- -

Holding Space Together

- What would global citizenship learning look and feel like at home to you, and how might this be different or similar to global citizenship learning abroad?
- What is different about being exposed to difference in far-off Togo or Botswana as a white Westerner with little experience with difference outside your mostly white community than, say, being exposed to difference in the closer to home but culturally quite different Mexican American or Black Canadian or Asian British communities that might be located ten or fifteen miles away?
- If you and Mandy were discussing her Cape Town experiences and she shared with you how she felt both abroad and at home with people of different races, how would you respond? What

are ways to be more socially bold and brave at home the way many of us feel abroad? What holds us back, and what might propel us through our discomfort even a little bit?

Suitcases Are Easy to Unpack. Journeys Take More Time

"I had a terrible time readjusting to life back home after my semester in Honduras," says a student of mine, a nineteen-year-old woman returning from her volunteer program. "It's not that people weren't nice to me or caring, it's just that I didn't know how to incorporate what I had learned back to my regular life. More than the learning of facts and figures, the learning I did abroad was actually relearning what I thought I knew about the world, about the reach and consequences of US foreign policy, about race, religion, about poverty. That's some tough stuff to process, so yeah, it takes time."

"It took me a long time to start processing my time abroad and to re-engage with it all," says another student who traveled to China as part of a service-learning program. "Learning so much in such a short amount of time needed to work through me in ways I didn't even know. With school, I'm used to studying, then knowing something, and then taking an exam to prove what I know. This trip has taught me in a really different way, and I've had to become more comfortable with this."

And says another student who studied abroad in India: "What I use from India most in my life now is a sense of care in how I approach ideas of social justice, development, travel, and entitlement. What stands out for me is the group of women we visited in that small village during the last week of the trip. I still think about them now, maybe once a week. I think about how vibrant and powerful they were. They remind me that happiness comes from feeling empowered to take control of your circumstances. I also still remember a question they asked us after they finished telling us about their lives. They asked, 'Is it like this where you come from?' I think that was a beautiful moment, and it gives me hope that cross-cultural travel can be productive. Our trip from six years ago still has a way of inserting itself back into my life in all kinds of ways."

As you think, reflect, write, and converse together, your insights may not come bounding toward you but might peek out and glimmer now and then. Our insights might also shift and change as we grow and become more of who we are. Deep learning is not instantaneous or fixed. Deep learning takes time, care, and commitment to unfold and cannot be rushed, even though we might be anxious to wrap up our thinking about our summer trip and move on to our fall classes. Breathing reminds us to make space for our feelings, memories, and questions about our travels.

Our journey from guilt to solidarity and action is predicated upon better understanding the ways that systems of power work in our lives. Our journeys, though, are also predicated upon holding close the moments of dignity, joy, resiliency, and connection that we witness and in which we take part. The real story of travel is not only evidenced in the official stamps of our passport or the colorful mementos we bring back from one global bazaar or another. Our traveling stories, rather, narrate what happens to us internally within our hearts, minds, and perspectives toward others. This is our nourishment, the meaningful souvenir. We take in many questions, merge them with bravery, and inch into small change when we talk about our vulnerabilities.

Our traveling stories don't end when we return, and if we're open, can guide our lives at home with more equity, intentionality, and meaningful conversations.

EPILOGUE

Night Here, Morning There

WHEN I AM TIRED AND WEARY, AND WHEN THE REPAIR OF OUR BROKEN world seems too daunting, I think of the many people I've met and read about who work for social change. I think about, for example, a group of Indian women I met a few years ago. These ordinary *and* amazing women challenged long-standing gendered stereotypes in their rural village and endured the wrath of male village elder power-holders for years, all while conscientiously caring for their families and each other with good humor, laughter, songs, and a driving spirit. They were, in effect, badass lady activists, the type of ladies who might never say they were activists, which made them glow even more brightly in their badassery.

I think of these women and the many other ordinary *and* amazing people around the world who ask critical questions about history, power, and opportunity, people who raise their fists and voices for justice. There are people in every corner of our earth who reject the business-as-usual thinking that grants power to too few of us. All kinds of changemaking folks—many in my own neighborhood as well as the many who live hundreds and thousands of miles away—make life better for others by creating new spaces of love, equity, and opportunity for more people.

Changemakers live in different pockets of the planet and come into the conversation with different identities. We all have roles to play. I am a changemaker. You might be one too. I know I am con-

nected to people around the world in an ongoing dance of night and morning, morning and night. Here's how I picture it: When it is morning for me, it is night somewhere else. When I wake in the morning, stretch, and begin my day, people in different pockets of the planet rest. I live my day well, and hopefully and in small ways, create spaces of love, equity, and opportunity for the people around me. Later that night when I fatigue, others for whom it is morning take over the global task of repair and change. They wake and stretch, and begin in their own ways to live well, and hopefully and in small ways, create spaces of love, equity, and opportunity in their own communities. When some of us wake, others rest, and when we rest, others wake. Night here, morning there. Morning here, night there.

This, to me, is what embodies global citizenship. Night here, morning there connects each of us to a roster of badassery, folks around the world who live near us, folks who we meet on our travels, and folks we hear about in the stories we share and the books we read. Within this worldwide community, we can all offer one another rest and hope as we forge links and make change. I think about these interconnections often, not only when I am weary of the work of repair and change, but also when I am feeling powerful about the meaningful conversations and connections we build together.

Author Mary Pipher tells us in *Writing to Change the World*, "Over the course of a lifetime, people who grow wiser—and not all of them do—expand their frames of reference and find themselves connected to more people and experiences. The best writers enlarge the points of view of their readers. They create overarching metaphors and build bigger frames that allow readers to understand this world more deeply."

Our journeys from the Global North to the Global South might not aim to make us all writers, but they do aim to make us more expansive thinkers and feelers. We rest-and-wake, wake-and-rest to make change and connect to each other meaningfully, and hopefully, with more grace, knowing that we are indeed similar in critically important ways, but never forgetting our critical differences as well.

Bigger frames, yes, strain and pain us, but also help us question what we know. Bigger frames mean we expand our circle of care, and complicate instead of simplifying. We open ourselves to understanding ourselves, our homes, and the larger world more deeply, even if the path is not always illuminated. As Gloria Anzaldúa reminds us, "Voyager, there are no bridges. One builds them as one walks."

ACKNOWLEDGEMENTS

I AM GRATEFUL FOR A WIDE NETWORK OF CONNECTIONS AND RELA-tionships that have supported my work in a variety of ways. I begin with Between the Lines Books, an awesome press deserving of much praise. I deeply appreciate managing editor Amanda Crocker's astute feel for what works and Mary Newberry's skillful and sensitive copy editing. Thanks also to BTL's Renée Knapp, David Molenhuis, and Devin Clancy, as well as Beate Schwirtlich, Jennifer Tiberio, and Maggie Earle.

At the University of Washington, Betty Schmitz was my first and best mentor on campus. Thanks to the English department for the home base from which to grow, the Study Abroad office for support-ing my programs, and CHID for its special hub of collegiality and the best lunchtime company in the U District.

Current and former UW colleagues I am grateful for: Adiam Tesfay, Amy Feldman-Bawarshi, Annie Fisher, Anis Bawarshi, Amy Peloff, Annie Dwyer, Ben Gardner, Beth Kalikoff, Brian Reed, Can-dice Rai, Carolyn Busch, Chanira Reang Sperry, Christine Stickler, Cynthia del Rosario, Darielle Horsey, David Fenner, Deepa Rao, Ed Taylor, Elisabeth Mitchell, Elizabeth Simmons-O Neill, Erin Clowes,

Fran Lo, Gary Handwerk, Jean Dennison, Jeanette James, Jen Self, Jessica McPherson, John Toews, Julie Villegas, July Hazard, Karla Tofte, Keith Snodgrass, Kimberlee Gillis-Bridges, Kristi Roundtree, Laine Noah, Laura Marquez, Lauren Easterling, LeAnne Wiles, Lorna Hamill, Manka Varghese, María Elena García, Miriam Bartha, Monica Rojas-Stewart, Nancy Sisko, Nara Hohensee, Nat Mengist, Natalie Lecher, Nighisty Habties, Peter Moran, Phillip Thurtle, Rachel Chapman, Rob Weller, Ron Krabill, Sasha Welland, Shawn Wong, Shirley Yee, Susan Williams, Suzanne St Peter, Tamara Myers, Theresa Ronquillo, Tikka Sears, Torie Reed, Ujima Donalson, and Vera Sokolova.

Many people have accompanied me on this manuscript journey directly and indirectly. My appreciation to Achashman Tekle, Amir Sheikh, Anusha Rao, Arathi Srikantaiah, Bani Amor, Beth Rayfield, Bookda Gheisar, Canh Tran, Carolyn Hall, Charmila Ajmera, Chen Lin, Christine Chaney, David Grosskopf, Dawn Marie Trouvé, DeAnn Alcantara-Thompson, Deb Gianola, Divya Ramachandra, Donna Austin, Francine Walker, Gary and Susan Hirayama, Guillermo Carvajal, Haley Doyle, Jabali Stewart, James Berry, John Vaughn, Kathryn Flores, Kathy Hsieh, Lisa Rice, Monique Brinson, Mary Pembroke-Perlin, Melanie Lorísdóttir, Minh Nguyen, Natasha Merchant, Nuansi Ngamsnit, Paj Nandi, Patrick Koppula, Peter Davenport, Rachelle Horner, Rafael Velázquez, Reid Von Pohle, Robin Wilcox, Ruby Lee, Saara Ahmed, Sam Hatzenbeler, Sandra Gresl, Sandy and Les Bartlett, Sarah Ann Wolf, Sarah Kislak, Scott Cleary, Serena Maurer, Shahana Dattagupta, Shaula Massena, Shila

Hodgins, Sonora Jha, Suzanne Greenberg, Tania Tam Park, Tanmeet Sethi, Tim Cahill, Tom Nolet, Uma Rao, Vikas Garg, Willy Oppenheim, Yani Robinson, Zahra Lutfeali, Zaki Barak Hamid, Pratama Nada music circle, and the WEB women.

Community partners around the world have helped me think about connecting across difference and traveling more mindfully. In India, I appreciate the longstanding friendship of B.N. Usha, Bhargavi S. Rao, Indhu Subramaniam, K.R. Mallesh, Radha Ramaswamy, Ravi Ramaswamy, and Somyashree Gonibeedu. I've learned from Abhayraj Naik's and Leo Saldanha's work and many social change advocates. In Mexico, thanks to our human rights partners Ari Vera, Carlos Ventura, Daniel Otero, Daniela Vázquez, Erandi Avendaño, Francisco Tenorio Hernández, Frida Amaro, Héctor Sánchez, Itzel Eguiluz, Jessica Durán Franco, Lía García, Lis Reséndiz, Lorna Zamora Robles, Marcela Tárano, Natalia Luna, Patricia López. Staff and associates of WARC West African Research Center in Dakar taught me firsthand about Senegalese hospitality and teranga, especially Ablaye Diakite, Adama Diouf, Marie Guèye, and Waly Faye. Partners in Accra, Ghana, have warmly welcomed me into their circle: Bright Kekeli Fiatsi, Douglas Opoku Agyemang, Emmanuel Ato Yamoah, Eric Opoku Agyemang, Freeman Ahegbebu, Nana Darkoa Sekyiamah, and Oppong Nyantakyi.

Deep appreciation to Anna Vodicka, Courtney De Vries, Darielle Horsey, Faith Adiele, Kathy Hsieh, Minal Hajratwala, Nayomi Munaweera, Rick Simonson, Vijay Prashad, and Willy Oppenheim for sending strategic introductions on my behalf. I am grateful to the reviewers for endorsing the book. Michelle Liu is a thinking partner and editor who can only be described as a treasure. She often knew what I was trying to say even before I did. Special thanks to illustrator Ronald "Otts" Bolisay for the many conversations on art and style and for the hexagon honeycomb.

Space at the Whiteley Center, a Hedgebrook residency, and a VONA fellowship granted me the gift of time and the opportunity to learn to feel like a writer.

I thank my lively extended kin in India and the US, including the Bungale, Ramachar, Taranath, Rao, Bhat, Kanjilal, and Kalkura families; PNAP Rao and Kamali Rao; niece and nephews Maya, Vijay, Rohan, Rahul, Mihir; Smitha, Deepak, Vaishali and Uday. My Amma Saroja, besides making the best akki roti and walnut chutney pudhi ever, is a great mother and grandmother, full of love and encouragement.

I miss the insights of three guides who are no longer with us: my graduate school mentor Rosemary George, elder-buddy Ramaswamy P.S., and father Bungale S. Taranath.

Thank you to Bookita Salon members and close friends Amy Hirayama, Bhavna Shamasunder, Brandon Maust, Cynthia Mumtaz Anderson, Emily Lee, Mala Nagarajan, Michelle Liu, Minh-Trâm Nguyen, Nicolaas Barr Clingan, Otts Bolisay, Rukie Thomas, Sahar Romani, Sasha Duttchoudhury, Shazia Rahman, Shirin Subhani, Suhanthie Motha, Tamera Marko, and Vega Subramaniam. Bhavna and Trâm are my GF squad. My love and gratitude to all the folks who make up GFW, Fruity, MASsiVe, Bikechick, ABA, KIKI, Pakkatata, Velcro, Boss, Ladies Coupe, and KARA.

I could never travel as much as I do without the constant support of my partner Rajesh Rao. Rajesh is truly an anchor for the family, filling our home with spirited conversation, well-studied art, and lots of humor.

My two kids Anika Tara and Kavi Ziya are my greatest cheerleaders. From Hatchling, Dragonita, OCR, and Banu-Pachuk to bum-da-lum, we have great fun with our nicknames and wacky wit. How lucky am I that such incredible humans call me Ammi!

APPENDIX

Especially for Educators, Program Directors, Leaders, and Coordinators

I'M IMAGINING THAT YOU AND I AND ANOTHER DOZEN OR SO OF OUR colleagues are sitting around a table with snacks and tea. We've gathered to discuss some of the most important issues facing us as educators who are involved in global studies in one way or another. Maybe we teach at a high school, community college, or take students abroad. We might work at an organization that links Western students with communities in the Global South, or maybe we are a consultant in the development field or a nurse who works with vulnerable populations. Though our careers span global health, secondary schools, the not-for-profit sector, and universities, we are aligned in our concern about the increasing corporatization of educational spaces. We strive to interrupt the for-profit business model that cares little about both our students' good intentions and civic engagement, as well as the long-term consequences for the communities abroad whose lack of resources and options keep them indebted to this form of Western aid. We're aligned in our passion for transformative education that speaks to the whole person from the inside out. We want to find ways to do our work more ethically and responsibly, less for the publicity or institutional kudos and more because if we can, we should.

What, then, is on our agenda? What do we want to discuss with one another? I've posed this question to colleagues over the years. Here are the topics that rise to the top, and what I'll briefly cover in this appendix.

- Politics of our field and our own positionality
- Demographics of who we work with and opportunities or critical angles we might be missing
- Skills we need as educators to stretch and grow our own comfort with uncomfortable topics
- Decisions we make in such a complicated terrain about staying or going

Politics and Our Positionality

Throughout my career, there's been one word that I admire more than any other, a word so small in terms of letters, yet so big in its capacity to hold multiple ideas at once—the word "and." The small and big word "and" helps us clearly see how two different ideas may be opposed and yet simultaneously true. Here's how "and" can help us better notice and grapple with the politics and complexities of our work:

- Many of us want to bridge historically produced differences through our global work, *and* much of global work reinforces historically produced difference.
- I love my career, *and* my career is ethically complicated (and sometimes, even ethically dubious).

- I work for social justice in many realms, *and* I am a part of systems that oppress others.
- Our good intentions are the sweetest thing ever, *and* our good intentions will never be enough.

Probably the most noticeable thing about each of these statements is the dissonance between the parts joined together by the *and*—dissonance with a dash of paradox, sprinkled with contradiction and vexation. This kind of *and* thinking implicates us, which makes us uncomfortable, but also has the potential to better us and broaden us as educators.

I'm not thrilled that the profession of which I am a part often thrives on the kinds of unchallenged and unchecked privileges I seek to deconstruct. A career centered on sensitizing Western students to issues of identity, global advantage, and power dynamics to challenge categories of difference and catalyze social change sounds great, but as noted throughout *Beyond Guilt Trips*, such a career also comes with its own deep complicities, challenges, and complexities. I am, in many ways, a part of the problem *and* the solution. To navigate the many inequities of our world more mindfully, I'll need a healthy combination of courage and grace to step toward the issues that make me uncomfortable. I'll definitely continue to feel things that are difficult to feel and process, but I don't want to drown in my own guilt. I also don't want to step away from this work because it's complicated; I'd rather learn how to better pilot my complicated feelings. Ironically, all my experience brings me both closer to better understanding how we travel across difference, and further away from feeling settled. The more I engage in these conversations, the more I grapple with my desire for social justice and the advantages that have offered me so much compared with many others. Here are the questions I continually ask myself that you too might find helpful:

- What are ways to lead my students in interactions with local people abroad in more mindful ways that do not turn away from the inequities of history that often structure our engagement with one another in the first place?
- How do my various identities—and my egotistical desire to be seen as a good person—figure in this? Am I a cultural insider, a native informant, or more bitingly, do I participate in cultural appropriation?
- How can I create authentic and caring relationships with my colleagues abroad while also acknowledging the incredible advantages I have via my US passport, more-than-most resources, and globe-trotting life?

Navigating paradox or dissonance—similar to other concepts like "sitting with discomfort" or "holding space for each other"—isn't really a skill we are taught, though it is critical to how we move through the world and interact with one another.

It's often helpful to consider examples of how others think of these ideas as a way to make our own sense of them. Here are ways that two scholars describe dissonance in their own work. In her 1993 book *Writing Diaspora: Tactics of Intervention in Contemporary Cultural Studies*, scholar Rey Chow offers an insightful and still extremely relevant take on the traffic in good intentions between the Global North and Global South, a traffic that is intimately tied to history and power:

> The difficulty facing us, it seems to me, is no longer simply the "first world" Orientalist who mourns the rusting away of his treasures, but also students from privileged backgrounds Western and non-Western, who conform behaviorally in every respect with the elitism of their social origins . . . but who nonetheless proclaim dedication to "vindicating the subalterns.". . . My point is not that they should be

blamed for the accident of their birth, nor that they cannot marry rich, pursue fame, or even be arrogant. Rather, it is that they choose to see in others' powerlessness an idealized image of themselves and refuse to hear in the dissonance between the content and manner of their speech their own complicity with violence. . . . they remain blind to their own exploitativeness as they make "the East" their career.

I love this quote for its acerbic quality, and how Chow precisely identifies the dissonance in our good intentions with regard to global "others." There's a very pointed critique in Chow's quote about our complicity in exploitation, and I think she's talking to you, and I think she's talking to me. We need to explore and discuss the dissonance between our desire to defend subalterns (our desire to do good and help others), and our own unconscious exploitativeness as we make careers in the metaphorical or literal "East."

Second example: A colleague of mine Suhanthie Motha is a scholar of English language teaching, which means she teaches people who want to teach English to other people. The English language, deeply intertwined with the history of colonialism, missionary work, racism, the "civilizing" project of Western education, and ideologies of empire, represents all the things that undercut Motha's core values of justice. She writes, "The challenge I face . . . is how to participate in English language teaching in a way that is responsible, ethical, and conscious of the consequences of our practice." Great question to also think about in terms of our own travels, study abroad programs, volunteering work, and teaching. Though we won't necessarily address all the problems inherent in our profession or come to neat conclusions about the unequal relationships in our own neighborhood or across the globe, the process itself of questioning and reflecting encourages us to hold and navigate the *and* parts of our lives. We are all part of the problem *and* solution.

- -

Holding Space Together

- Write down four to five *and* statements that reflect your current job description, role, professional interests, or field. What paradoxes, dissonance, or contradictions are being held by the small-yet-big word *and* in your statements?
- Does your field or professional community address these issues? If so, in what ways? If not, why do you think not? What are meaningful ways you might convene a conversation on some of these issues with your colleagues or in a PLC, a professional learning community?

- -

Our Students, Who Are They?

In "Katherine and Ali," the story I told early in *Beyond Guilt Trips*, where the nine private college students visit the urban high school, all the college students are white, and all the high school students are people of color. How would this interaction have played out differently if, say, the college students were majority students of color of varying ethnicities and cultures? I wonder how their presentation on Togo, their informal mentorship of the high school students, and the broader conversation of going somewhere far to learn about diversity, might have resonated differently or similarly with the high school students. Perhaps the college students of color would not have felt as awkward and uncomfortable in classroom. Or perhaps they would have still felt awkward and uncomfortable, but for entirely different reasons than their white peers. It's difficult to know any of this for sure, though it's essential to at least consider alternatives outside of the usual narrative.

Beyond the high school visit, I wonder how this college group's travels through Togo might also play out differently if they were a group of majority students of color. Though I'm using broad categories of "white students" and "students of color" to provoke critical thinking and inspire discussion—there is no one "white experience" or "person of color experience." We've got a range of heterogeneity and experiential diversity in all groups of people, even if they do share racial characteristics. That being said, we also know that all of us experience different realities of our identities through the axes of race, power, access, degrees of belonging, and traveling through difference both closer to home as well as far away.

While all kinds of students can benefit from going abroad and learning about themselves and the world, we need to notice which students are seen as getting the most benefits from exposure to the qualities of global citizenship. According to NAFSA, the Association of International Educators, at 70 percent, white students comprise the majority of study abroad program participants in the United States. In some schools, colleges, and universities the percentage is even higher, and doesn't even cover the hundreds of thousands of young people going abroad every year in other kinds of volunteer, missionary, service learning, and development programs. This over-representation of white students is both understandable and concerning: understandable, because growing up many white young people are encouraged and empowered to "explore the world" through the recommendations of their parents, teachers, counselors, and other well-resourced adults. White over-representation on study abroad and other travel programs, though, is concerning because these numbers correlate to the under-representation of students of color.

Remember the earlier discussion on residential segregation and the lack of well-integrated, mixed-race, and mixed-class neighborhoods across America? When we say we want our study abroad students to "increase their familiarity with diversity" by going abroad, we seem to be saying we want our white students to be more comfortable with people of different races and economic levels. This is fine as far as it goes—but it's not very far. Prioritizing this as the exclusive goal eclipses two critical points. First, rather than encourage students to go abroad to learn about issues of diversity, equity, and social justice, we need to look more closely at issues of diversity, equity, and social justice in our communities at home and ask questions about *who* are getting *what* opportunities and *why*. In chapter 9, Mandy's experience of feeling bold to speak with Black South African students abroad and less comfortable engaging with African Americans in her hometown speaks to this tension between what we're ostensibly sending students abroad to learn and what we're not properly addressing at home. Second, because students of color on our programs are often being offered pedagogical opportunities based on our understanding of white students' identities and needs, we have to rethink what our goals are and for whom.

The other side of the statistical model we are all working in is that about 30 percent of study abroad participants are students of color, a number that many initiatives across the country seek to raise. Too often, though, programmatic goals implicitly align themselves to the cultural experiences of economically privileged students, most (but not all) of whom are white. White students (and in smaller percentages, high-income people of color), mostly raised in majority white communities, are presumed to have little experience with racial and economic "diversity" (a term I have encased in scare quotes since it's not clear what we actually mean by it). Meanwhile, what about the 28 percent who are students of color and the various experiences they already inhabit? (We can ask the same questions about other students as well, our working-class, low-income, gender fluid, transgender, students with disabilities, and/or first-generation students).

If we centered the identities, experiences, and learning of students of color and other students often left out of the mainstream, I wonder how program offerings and the language used to advertise our goals might shift.

For example, students of color may well have had different racialized experiences in their lives than their white peers. Perhaps these students' "familiarity with diversity and multiculturalism" or "comfort zones" related to diversity might look and feel different than our default understanding of white students. Since many young people of color must daily travel through and grapple with the white world as well as their own home cultures, their experiences of "navigating difference and diversity" might look and feel distinct from their white classmates. Additionally, because the mainstream world of higher education often is normalized to be white space, some students of color attending these institutions *already feel* like they've traveled quite far away from their home cultures just doing regular things like living in on-campus housing, going to class, or studying at the library. As travel writer Faith Adiele says, "People of color are the most traveled people on the planet; every time we leave our houses, we travel." How then, do we teach to *all* our students instead of catering only to the most culturally dominant and demographically strong group? I don't have one answer for this. It gets complicated to talk about "all white students" or "all students of color" because, as we've said before, there isn't only one kind of this or that student. White students are not a monolithic entity any more than are students of color. And yet, most of our programs are organized *as if* our students are a monolithic bunch. We as teachers have to stretch our own comfort zones and become better adept at noticing and naming who our programs are peopled with and why.

Stretching and Growing Our Discomfort Zones

Leading a program outside your home community isn't only about managing the logistics of accommodations, meals, and excursions. Leading a program means managing young people's lives and their interaction with the long history and present manifestations of inequality and all that this entails. As educators we will go a long way if we can learn to talk about these issues meaningfully with our students and especially about experiences that are outside our own. That we don't know how to begin or sustain conversations on issues of identity, difference, and power is not because we're bad people, but because we live in a racialized society that to consolidate and maintain power has purposefully kept us fearful, nervous, and silent. That is the business-as-usual model. The more we're anxious and silent, the more the prevailing structure remains intact.

When I facilitate program director workshops and seminars in different parts of the United States, I am with rooms full of sincere white educators (sprinkled with a few educators of color) who are

looking for ways to deepen their pedagogical impact with their students. These educators have had few opportunities to engage in the kinds of conversations that ask questions about upbringings, socialization, and epistemological frameworks (how we know what we know). I don't have figures for this, but I'm guessing that the majority of program directors, field coordinators, and leaders who shepherd Western students to the Global South are similar to those I've met over the years: white and relatively economically well-off who have grown up with certain social advantages. It makes sense that these educators are less comfortable with topics of identity and difference; those who are closer to the mythical norms have often had less need to actively investigate the power structures they are a part of, no matter how well-intentioned.

If we've not had adequate opportunity to safely investigate *our own* racial identity or class location or gendered experience without the usual shame, blame, and guilt, how will we know how to model this for our students? Without critically investigating how we ourselves came to be who we are in an unequal world, how can we confidently facilitate our students through the murky terrain of these conversations and recuperate when things get difficult?

We can take advantage of professional development and training opportunities—they are out there and we can use more. And we can work to deepen ourselves as people in the world so we can deepen our impact as educators.

- -

Teachers Need to Learn, Too

 Program directors, group leaders, and teachers—like student travelers—aren't always sure how to navigate issues of race, identity, and systems of power as they relate to them or their students abroad. A colleague of mine, a white woman program leader in her mid-forties named Jane, tells me about a disturbing moment on her recent study abroad program to Germany. One day, she and her students spent an afternoon browsing colorful wares in a Berlin street market. Pairs of students fanned across the market area, and my colleague found herself next to her twenty-year-old Japanese American student Aiko. The two convivially walked together and stopped at a stall to look around. The shopkeeper of the stall, a middle-aged Turkish man, looked at Aiko and began to make loud comments and big gestures directed at her. Though he was speaking in Turkish and neither Aiko nor Jane could understand what he was saying, it seemed he was perturbed about Aiko's Asianness. Or at least, that's what they both thought as they hurried away.

Aiko, predictably, was shaken up. Never having been the target of overt racism in the United States, she could not fathom why this man had denigrated her so, especially given the anti-Muslim and anti-immigrant sentiments prevalent in Germany of which the shopkeeper himself might have been the recipient. If his reaction had indeed been about her race, Aiko couldn't understand how a non-white person of color might espouse prejudice toward another non-white person of color. Jane, too, wasn't sure how to unpack the situation. Was this instance really about Aiko's race or something else? Was it about her gender or her Americanness? How could either of them be sure?

Jane wonders, "As an older white woman, how do I support Aiko around this moment, and more generally, my other students of color abroad? I don't want to trivialize these kinds of incidents, but I also don't know what to do as the program director. I feel ill-equipped to bring it up. I don't know what it's like to be a person of color either at home or abroad. What if I make the situation worse?" Though Jane's own identity means she hasn't had to deal with issues of race in the same ways as people of color might have, Jane *is* a great educator, and she cares deeply about the participants on her program. She feels bad for the student, bad about her own deficiencies, and bad about racism (if this instance, was, indeed about race). Here's a range of questions focused on pedagogy, curriculum, and critical approaches to identity and difference. If the status quo isn't working for all our students, how might we stretch and shift as educators and program directors?

Holding Space Together

- If you found yourself in a situation similar to Jane's with her student Aiko, how might you approach your student? I'm thinking in terms of your approach to a student as being less in the role of a fully confident expert and more to lend the support of a sympathetic ear.
- Would you bring up the incident with the rest of the students? Why or why not?
- What kinds of difference or diversity do we want our students of color to become more comfortable with abroad (and perhaps at home too), and how might that be similar or different to the kinds of difference or diversity we want our white students to become more comfortable with? What about our gender fluid students? Working-class or first generation students?
- How are we working to decolonize our programs so that they are more inclusive of different kinds of students *and* so they expand what is traditionally discussed?
- Think back to the story in chapter 3 where Niya, a student studying in the Dominican Republic, is barred from entering a club because of her hair. If you were the program leader on this trip and learned of the incident, how would you bring it up with Niya? How about with the two students who were with her? How might we facilitate conversation with the entire group to make space and hold the moment so Niya feels heard *and* everyone has an opportunity to reflect on broader issues of beauty, belonging, and bias that we all constantly navigate?

Training to Be Bolder and Better Educators

In a workshop about the role of diversity in international education, a colleague critiques the "add some color to look more progressive" model of diversity. Mainstream diversity rhetoric, she says, isn't actually about encouraging us to rethink what we do and how. It's simply about showcasing a student of color or a student in a wheelchair on an official website or program brochure to make it seem that the institution is paying attention to all its students. "Yes, these students certainly matter," she says, "and our media and imagery should reflect the range of students we work with. But the way institutions use these kinds of photos feels like window-dressing and needs to be reconsidered."

"But what are the ethics and responsibility of leading minority students abroad?" one of the white men asks. He leads programs to China and Nepal. "People around the world differentiate each other based on prejudice and racism. None of us can be responsible for what happens abroad. It makes me nervous to encourage students of color to join my program and guarantee that they won't be offended by something that takes place abroad."

"We won't be able to guarantee anything abroad, similarly to how we cannot guarantee anything closer to home," says a white woman who leads programs to Rome and Florence in Italy.

"We cannot guarantee anything anywhere," another white woman faculty member emphatically states. "But we can learn how to talk about what happens and may happen to better support all our students abroad."

Holding Space Together

- What kinds of conversations on identity, diversity, advantage, privilege, history, and access are you having at your workplace or organization? How is it going? What feels difficult about the discussions, and what feels honest? What kind of training, workshop, information, or tools would be most helpful to you and the people around you, and why?
- If you're based in an institution like a school, college, or university, take some time to look at the official imagery on its website and promotional materials. What do you notice? What might be missing or invisibilized to those who typically see people like themselves in the media?

"Doing diversity," at least in *Beyond Guilt Trips* and in my work, isn't only about counting how many of whom. It's about fundamentally rethinking how we're doing things from start to finish, and expecting that we'll be asking tough questions along the way. What this means for you and me as educators, program directors, and guides is that we'll have to get more practiced at creating space for such conversations with our colleagues and using the space wisely. We'll have to get better at noticing what's happening in our literal classrooms at home, and abroad in the field, the classrooms we create with our excursions, discussions, and site visits. We'll also need to get better at encouraging our students to engage in the kinds of reflective writing and project work that help them ask and grapple with big questions. To open spaces for our students to be more nimble and flexible—more stretchable in their thinking—we as educators too will have to open those spaces for ourselves.

Three Resources: Encouraging Students to Think Differently

 Here are three resources developed by me with under-graduate student collaborators with practical exercises that creatively encourage critical thinking and travel across difference. I have found them to be useful exercises and prompts in many situations—you may also find them helpful with your own students, or even in your next faculty pedagogy workshop, program staff development workshop, or curriculum committee meeting:

1) *TIPS to Study Abroad: Simple Letters for Complex Engagement* showcases a letter-writing assignment I developed during a study abroad program in India. The weekly letters focused on "TIPS," an acronym for Things, Ideas, People and Self. The letters that my students produced were funny, insightful, poignant, and provocative. Here's a sample of to what or whom the students wrote letters:

Dear Plastic Water Bottles
Dear Generosity
Dear Girl I Read About in the Papers who was Bitten by
    a Snake and Died
Dear Chai Breaks in the Middle of Class
Dear Village Leader who Organized a Protest with 1000
    People and 4000 Sheep
Dear Myself Before I Came to India
Dear Myself After I Go Home
Dear Poop!

The letters my students wrote were amazing, not only because they nicely captured the cacophony of sights, sounds, smells, and people that is India, but also because they saw the assignment as a space to navigate the identity issues that traveling abroad frequently raises. My students, like many Westerners visiting the Global South for the first time, found their previous understandings about race, sexuality, gender, poverty, privilege, and access to be inadequate and unsatisfactory. By contrast, the weekly ritual of handwriting TIPS letters provided a focused and almost meditative space for students to reflect on what they had experienced and how they felt changed, challenged, or fortified. Despite its small local roots, *TIPS to Study Abroad* has been adopted by a wide assortment of organizations, institutions and educators to offer a new model of critical global engagement.

2) *Let's WOW It Out: Simple Drawings to Explore Big Ideas* presents an assignment that moves us from the textual to the visual. "WOW" stands for Word of the Week. Each week I gave students a tremendously complex concept to consider—racism, colonialism, resistance, for example— and asked them to *draw* their understanding of the word and its many dimensions. I created this assignment as a way to interrupt the academy's overreliance on words, and to encourage students to engage with broad concepts from a more creative angle. WOWers, as we called ourselves, did not have to be artists. In fact, drawing skills became secondary as we focused on freeing our minds from the stifling "I can't draw" messages many of us tell ourselves, and instead, concentrated on illustrating and artfully

representing big concepts. Because images are differently accessible than the ten- or fifteen-page papers students were producing for their other classes, students enthusiastically shared their WOW drawings with parents, grandparents, younger siblings and relatives, roommates, and friends. Across the board, WOW drawings inspired all kinds of people to ask questions, engage, and discuss critical issues with one another.

3) The third publication, *The Q-SAR, Queer Study Abroad Resource*, is a full-color, online travel resource highlighting photography and personal narratives of queer and nonqueer US undergraduates studying abroad in Mexico and navigating their identity. Drawn from interviews, focus groups, and reflective writing prompts, the testimonies highlighted throughout the resource model the kinds of conversations and discussions that interrupt business-as-usual awkwardness and silence. *The Q-SAR* provides a focused space for travelers to consider identity in relation to sexuality and gender and creates bridges of understanding by sharing stories with one another.

Should We Stay or Should We Go

Simply going somewhere different doesn't necessarily open any of us to new ways of thinking. Nor does a longer plane ride automatically make a global citizen out of our students or us. While our educational institutions encourage hundreds and thousands of Westerners to go elsewhere, ultimately, this might not be what global citizenship and a better engagement with diversity issues is actually about. This process of becoming a global citizen really depends on how we think of identities, differences in experience and the dynamics of power, how and why we go elsewhere, what we do there, and how we incorporate this knowledge back home into our lives.

I have returned from every one of my international trips wholly unprepared to celebrate my newfound global citizenship. I often return home with more questions than answers, less sure of many more things. I feel so grateful for the opportunities I've received but remain deeply vexed about the privileges that educational travel affords some of us. I want to cultivate in myself, in my students, and in other educators a conscientious and critical lens that helps us see our present with an eye toward the past, and a lens that helps us ask "Why?" and "How come?" This lens, I've found, isn't like a pair of sunglasses I sport on a particularly bright afternoon and then remove at dusk. Rather, the kind of lens I'm advocating stays on our retinas for much longer. It's an internal lens that affects how we interact with our outside.

To hold our good intentions along with the complexities of identity and difference I've outlined throughout *Beyond Guilt Trips*, we do not, let me be clear, tell our students to stay at home. We do not not-go abroad out of a misplaced sense of guilt for all that we have access to or because it feels safer, less complicated, or too problematic. Guilt—even the well-meaning variety that hopes to motivate change—does not fundamentally change or help explain who has what opportunity or why. If a Western traveler simply frets over the privileges they have and, consequently, declines the opportunity to go to Liberia, Botswana, or Honduras, we can ask—Does the decision to not-go change the broader global context of inequity? Does the decision contribute to positive change? In partial answer, Richard Slimback writes in his book *Becoming World Wise: A Guide to Global Learning,* "At the end of the day, we must concede the disturbing fact that we live in this world at each other's expense. Our affluence as world learners is proximately related to, and supported by, the poverty of those who host us. Guilt isn't useful for this, and neither is saying 'it's too complex' which serves as an alibi and surrender."

While I think it's important to not not-go out of guilt, I also don't think we should encourage our students to go abroad cavalierly—just because we can. Yes, for some of us the world is accessible and at our fingertips, but that privilege can too easily go to our heads. Just because some of us have numerous opportunities to go abroad, should we? Critical questions provide an avenue to slow down our enthusiasm and consider what exactly is at stake and for whom. As Westerners with different experiences of privilege, let's dial down our global entitlement and realize there are consequences to where we go, what we do, and how we go. While staying home out of guilt helps nobody, a trip abroad with no critical engagement with issues of power, history, identity, and difference is also ethically bankrupt. Instead, let's create more educational spaces where we can learn about and discuss how we

- notice our advantages
- notice other people's experiences
- contextualize the past
- make sense of the present
- think about and work for justice
- make space for difference
- reflect on our interconnections

It's time for a change. Let's talk more about why some communities near us and countries far from us have so much or so little, and how that feels deep in our hearts. Let's talk more about what the true accounting of difference and equity really looks like in our schools, universities, neighborhoods, and workplaces. If we pretend that we're fine on the outside but quake with discomfort on the inside for what we have, who we are, or what we've had access to in our lives, we simply perpetuate more guilt trips. Instead, why not take a few deep breaths, say the things we notice out loud, and learn how to navigate the structures and hierarchies we've inherited in more productive ways? You or I can't fully upend the bigger story of unfair power. In small ways, though, we can interrupt the force of business-as-usual by acknowledging what's in front of us and relearning how to be in relationship with ourselves and each another.

Just consider: it's a crowded planet. Why not learn to cultivate a global traveling lens that helps us look at the complexities and layers that are all around us, both far away and closer to home? If the unexamined life is not worth living, the unexamined trip might not be worth taking either.

INDEX

Morrison, Toni, 1
Motha, Suhanthie, 209
Mozambique, 147, 185
multiculturalism, 37, 76, 213
music videos, 98
mythical norm, 48–58, 68, 82–83,
  92, 98, 111, 122, 133, 187, 215

NAFSA (Association of International Educators), 211
naming, 42–43, 44, 157, 213
National Volunteer Week, 2
nativism, 56
negativity, 168
neo-colonialism, 129
neo-imperialism, 115
Nepal, 218
New Zealand, 120
Nicaragua, 30
niceness, culture of, 56
non-governmental organizations
  (NGOs), 2
non-profits, 2
normality, 51, 64
norms: cultural, 125; racial and
  ethnic, 98; social, 106. *See also*
  mythical norms
noticing, 42–43, 44, 47, 53, 111,
  124, 224
novelty, 40

Omprakash, 191
openness, 11, 13, 31, 53
Oppenheim, Willy, 191
opportunity, 4, 141, 147, 149,
  160, 167, 175–76, 184, 193,
  223; access to, 56, 59, 153; differences in, 43, 161; economic,
  32; gaps in, 156; structural
  forces of, 184; systemic, 114
oppression, 53, 83, 188, 207;
  internalized, 106; structural, 1

ordinariness, 51–54, 64, 70, 92,
  173
ostracism, 4
out-groups, 14–17; discrimination
  against, 14–15

Pakistan, 89, 184, 187
Palmer, Parker: *The On Being
  Project*, 164
paradox, 207–8
Parker, Pat: "To the White Person
  Who Wants to be My Friend," 14
past: contextualizing, 224; unequal
  dynamics of, 124
patience, 70, 193
patriarchy, 28, 32, 48, 54, 91, 98,
  100, 114
paying attention, 43
pedagogy, 191, 216
personal learnings, 43–44
Peru, 126–29, 133, 138
Philippines, 96; colonialism
  and, 115
physical differences, 13, 19, 101.
  See also skin color
Pipher, Mary: *Writing to Change
  the World*, 203
Pitt, William Rivers: "Tip Your
  Server and Save the World," 186
pity, 149
platitudes, surface, 118–21
police profiling, 124
police surveillance, 32
politeness, 12, 47
political campaigns, 177
political histories, 30
politics: as local, 188; and positionality, 206–10
Portugal: colonialism and, 115
Portuguese, 74–76, 81
positionality, 113, 125; global,
  138; and politics, 206–10

Photograph by Quinn R. Brown

DR. ANU TARANATH brings both passion and expertise to her work as a speaker, facilitator, and educator. A professor at the University of Washington, she teaches about global literatures, race, gender, identity, and equity. A four-time member of Humanities Washington Speakers Bureau, Dr. Anu has also received *Seattle Weekly*'s "Best of Seattle" recognition, the UW's Distinguished Teaching Award, and multiple US Fulbright Fellowships to work abroad. As a racial equity consultant and facilitator, Dr. Anu engages with colleges, community organisations, businesses, and government agencies to deepen people's comfort with uncomfortable topics and work toward equity and social justice. More at www.anutaranath.com.